"To all the hustlers out there, grinding day and night to turn their passions into profits, this book is for you. May it be the guide that helps you turn your side hustle into your main hustle. Cheers to making money and living life on our own terms."

20 PRACTICAL WAYS TO GENERATE EXTRA INCOME

A STEP-BY-STEP GUIDE TO MAKE SIDE HUSTLE WHILE KEEPING YOUR FULL-TIME GIG

DR. ABHIJEET BIRARI

Copyright © Dr. Abhijeet Birari
All Rights Reserved.

This book has been self-published with all reasonable efforts taken to make the material error-free by the author. No part of this book shall be used, reproduced in any manner whatsoever without written permission from the author, except in the case of brief quotations embodied in critical articles and reviews.

The Author of this book is solely responsible and liable for its content including but not limited to the views, representations, descriptions, statements, information, opinions and references ["Content"]. The Content of this book shall not constitute or be construed or deemed to reflect the opinion or expression of the Publisher or Editor. Neither the Publisher nor Editor endorse or approve the Content of this book or guarantee the reliability, accuracy or completeness of the Content published herein and do not make any representations or warranties of any kind, express or implied, including but not limited to the implied warranties of merchantability, fitness for a particular purpose. The Publisher and Editor shall not be liable whatsoever for any errors, omissions, whether such errors or omissions result from negligence, accident, or any other cause or claims for loss or damages of any kind, including without limitation, indirect or consequential loss or damage arising out of use, inability to use, or about the reliability, accuracy or sufficiency of the information contained in this book.

Made with ♥ on the Notion Press Platform
www.notionpress.com

Contents

Foreword

As the publisher of "20 Practical Ways to Generate Extra Income", I can confidently say that this book is a game-changer for anyone looking to boost their income. From the moment I read the manuscript, I knew it was something special.

The author has done an outstanding job of researching and compiling a comprehensive list of income-generating methods that are practical, actionable, and easy to understand. Each chapter is packed with valuable information, from tips and tricks to real-life success stories that will inspire and motivate readers to take action.

What sets this book apart is its versatility. The author has included a wide range of methods, from traditional ways of earning extra income like freelancing and stock trading, to more unconventional methods like becoming a delivery executive and participating in paid online surveys. This means that regardless of your interests or skill set, you're sure to find a method that works for you.

Additionally, the author's casual and relatable writing style makes the book a pleasure to read. The author has a way of explaining complex concepts in simple terms, making it accessible to readers of all levels of experience.

I highly recommend "20 Practical Ways to Generate Extra Income" to anyone looking to increase their income. It's a valuable resource that will provide readers with the tools and inspiration they need to achieve their financial goals.

This book is also great for those who are looking for ways to make money from the comfort of their own home. From starting a blog or YouTube channel, to creating an online course or selling handmade items, there are plenty of options for those who want to work from home.

One of my favorite things about this book is that it doesn't just give you a list of options, but it also provides a step-by-step guide on how to get started with each method. From setting up a website for your blog to creating a course outline, the author has thought of everything to make the process as smooth as possible.

Another great thing about this book is that it doesn't just focus on one type of audience. It is meant for everyone, whether you are a student, a housewife, a retiree or a working professional, everyone can benefit from the ideas mentioned in the book.

And last but not the least, this book comes with a money-back guarantee, that is, if you don't make extra income after implementing the ideas from the book, you can return it and get your money back (Just Kidding, it's not that type of book) But in all seriousness, this book is a must-read for anyone looking to increase their income and achieve financial freedom.

In short, this book is a treasure trove of income-generating ideas and a must-read for anyone looking to boost their income. So, what are you waiting for? Grab a copy and start making some extra cash today!

Preface

Hey there!

Thanks for picking up "20 Practical Ways to Generate Extra Income"! This book is packed with information and inspiration to help you take control of your finances and start earning more money.

Let's be real, who doesn't love a little extra cash? Whether you're looking to pay off debt, save for a vacation, or just have some extra spending money, this book is for you. Inside, you'll find 20 different ways to start earning extra income today.

Now, I know what you might be thinking, "But I don't have a business idea or any special skills." That's totally fine! In this book, you'll find a wide variety of ways to earn extra income, from starting a blog or YouTube channel to renting out your car to freelancing and selling homemade or handmade items. We'll also take a look at some more unconventional methods of earning extra income, such as becoming a delivery executive, participating in paid online surveys, and getting paid to answer questions. And, of course, we'll explore the world of affiliate marketing and network marketing.

One of the things I love about this book is that it's not just about making money, it's about turning your passions and skills into profitable endeavors. Whether you're a stay-at-home parent looking for a way to earn some extra money, or a recent college grad seeking to start your own business, you'll find the information and inspiration you need to get started.

In this book, you'll find practical tips, actionable advice, and real-life success stories to help you get started on your journey. And, the best part? You can pick and choose which methods work best for you. You don't have to do them all!

So, grab a cup of coffee, get comfy and let's dive in! I'm excited to share all these ways to generate extra income with you and help you take control of your finances. Let's make it happen!

Acknowledgements

We would like to extend our deepest gratitude to the Director of Christ University, Pune, Lavasa campus Dr. Fr Jossy P George for his unwavering support and guidance throughout the creation of this book. We would also like to thank the Academic Coordinator Fr Justin P Verghese for his invaluable contributions. We are grateful to our colleagues in the department for their support and encouragement throughout the process. Our friends and students have also been a great source of inspiration and motivation. Last but not the least, we would like to thank our families for their love, support and understanding. Without them, this book would not have been possible.

Prologue

The world is constantly changing and evolving, and with it, so are the ways in which we can make a living. Gone are the days when a traditional 9-5 job was the only option for financial stability. Now, there are countless opportunities to earn an income through creative and innovative means.

This book is a guide to 20 Practical Ways to Generate Extra Income. From blogging and car rentals, to stock trading and creating online courses, these methods have been tried and tested by real people, who have not only found financial success, but also the satisfaction of turning their passions into profitable ventures.

Whether you're looking for a side hustle to supplement your income, or the inspiration to start your own business, this book has something for everyone. It's not just about making money, it's about taking control of your financial future and finding the path that's right for you.

So, let's dive in and explore the many ways in which you can start earning extra income today. Who knows, you might just discover your next big idea.

ONE
YOUTUBE CHANNEL

I am sure that all of you must have YouTube App on your mobile phone and must be using it frequently to watch the videos. The YouTube has variety of videos like educational videos, how to videos, whiteboard videos, product reviews, unboxing videos, explainer videos etc.

Have you ever wondered why these video creators must be spending hours of their time on researching, script writing, shooting, editing and publishing? What is in it for them on YouTube? You guessed it right. Money!!!

The content creators on YouTube generate income from variety ways but before I explain you how you can also generate income from YouTube, let me show you estimated earnings of popular Indian YouTubers in rupees, as of September 2021.

1. Gaurav Chaudhary, Rs. 326 crores
2. Amit Bhadana, Rs. 47 crores
3. Nisha Madhulika, Rs. 33 crores
4. Carry Minati, Rs. 29 crores
5. Ashish Chanchlani, Rs. 29 crores
6. Bhuvan Bam, Rs. 22 crores
7. Sandeep Maheshwari, Rs. 22 crores
8. Emiway Bantai, Rs. 18 crores
9. Harsh Beniwal, Rs. 16 crores
10. Vidya Vox, Rs. 9 crores

Now, you must be wondering how do these "YouTubers" make money from YouTube? There are 4 major ways through which they make money.

1. **YouTube partner program**: You might have seen various types of ads (Figure 1) while browsing YouTube. Whenever your video is viewed, a part of revenue goes to the creator of the video.

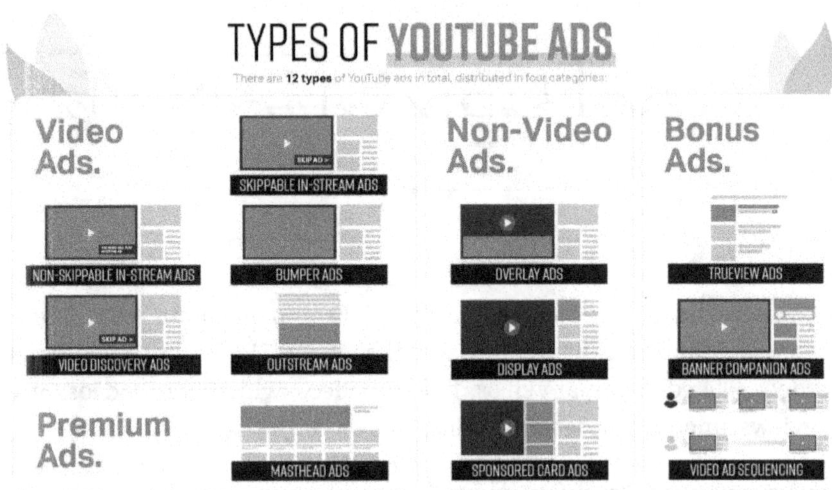

Types of Ads on YouTube

YouTube Partners have access to multiple income streams: not just video ads, but YouTube Premium subscription fees, and features that tap your loyal fans' wallets directly like Super Chat, channel memberships and the merchandise shelf. To earn money through partner program, you must have a YouTube Channel and need a minimum of 1,000 subscribers and 4,000 watch hours in the previous 12 months. Since this is the most common way of making money through YouTube, a step-by-step by guide is provided in this chapter later.

2. **Create sponsored content**: You don't have to be on Instagram to be an influencer. The advantage of this is that you don't have to give YouTube a cut of your earnings. You negotiate directly with the brand, and they pay you directly. No wonder it's a popular way for YouTubers to make money. For example, you make videos on investment so you can partner with financial institutions like broking firms, insurance companies, banks, fintech companies to promote their product/services through your videos.

3. **Become an affiliate partner**: If your YouTube audience is loyal and engaged, but not quite there yet headcount-wise, look for companies investing in affiliate marketing. YouTubers affiliated with businesses encourage their viewers to visit the brand's online store or specific product pages. They then get a percentage of sales made through their — you guessed it — affiliate links.

4. **Get your fans to pay you directly**: YouTube offers the ability to let your viewers pay you to become members of your channel. In exchange, they get custom emoji, badges, and access to members-only exclusives like Live Chats with you. Refer to this membership program on TechnicalGuruji channel.

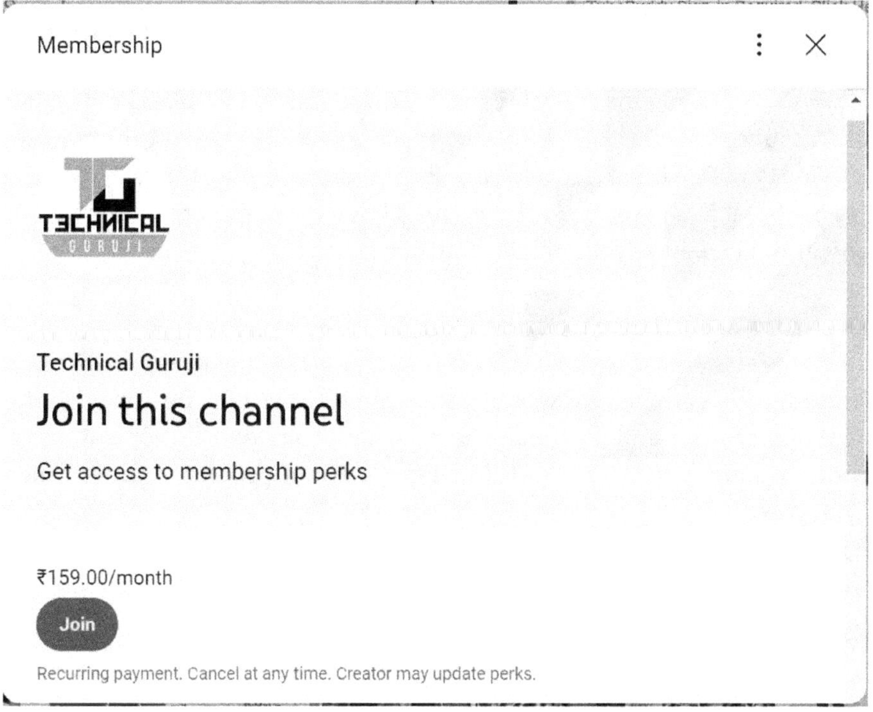

Membership Program on YouTube

With an exceptional strategy and pure dedication, you can turn YouTube into a legitimate career-building platform. People are making tons of money producing YouTube videos every day. If you're wondering how to start a

YouTube channel and make money from it, then you've come to the right place!

Why YouTube?

YouTube has become one of the most popular social media platforms in the world, with over 2 billion monthly active users. This video-sharing platform not only allows people to share their creativity and passions, but also provides an opportunity to make money. Content creators can earn revenue through various methods, including ad revenue, sponsorships, merchandise sales, and more. As a result, making money on YouTube has become a viable career option for many people. In this day and age, where the digital space is constantly growing and evolving, creating content for YouTube has become an increasingly accessible way to reach a wide audience and monetize your passions.

Now, all this sounds really great, but how to start a YouTube channel and make money?

Well, you don't need to be tech-savvy to know how to create a YouTube channel. Just head over to YouTube.com, sign in to your Google account, and boom! You now have your official YouTube channel.

Creating a YouTube Channel

Honestly, you can make anything and become famous on YouTube, as long as you're creative and passionate about what you're doing. People watch a wide variety of videos on YouTube. Here's a list of popular YouTube video categories:

- Singing
- Teaching
- Tutorials
- Fashion Advice
- Make-Up Tutorials
- Cooking Videos
- Pet Videos
- Comedy Videos
- Tech Videos
- Product Reviews

- How To Tutorials and Guides
- Video Game Walkthroughs
- Vlogs
- Celebrity Gossips
- Unboxing Videos
- Comedy or Sketch Videos
- Shopping Sprees
- Prank Videos
- Parodies

Step-by-Step Guide to Start YouTube Channel

Creating a YouTube channel can be an exciting and fulfilling adventure, but it can also feel overwhelming, particularly if you're inexperienced with the platform. Beginning a successful YouTube channel requires an understanding of the necessary steps involved. In this guide, we'll outline the essential stages required to start a YouTube channel, from determining your niche and establishing your channel to uploading your first video and promoting your content. Whether your goal is to share your enthusiasm for cooking, gaming, or any other topic, this step-by-step guide will provide you with the tools you need to get started and set you on the path to achievement.

1. The first step in creating a YouTube channel is to have a Google account. If you don't already have one, you can create one by going to the Google account creation page and following the prompts. If you already have a Google account, you can use that to set up your YouTube channel.
2. Once you are logged in to your Google account, go to the YouTube website. On the top right corner of the page, you will see a "Sign In" button. Click on it.
3. After clicking the sign in button, you will be taken to a page where you can create your YouTube channel. Click on the "Create a Channel" button to start the process.
4. Give your channel a name that represents your content and select a category that best describes it. The name you choose will be the title of your channel and will be visible to all viewers.

5. To customize your channel, you can add a profile picture, banner, and description. These elements will help your channel stand out and make it more attractive to potential viewers.

6. After you have filled in all the necessary information, click the "Create Channel" button to finish setting up your YouTube channel.

7. Now that your channel is set up, you can start uploading videos. To do this, click on the camera icon on the top right corner of the YouTube page.

8. Optimize your video by giving it a title, description, and tags. These elements will help viewers find your video when searching for content on YouTube.

9. Use YouTube analytics to understand your audience and improve your content. Analytics will provide you with information about your viewers, such as their age, gender, and location.

10. Promote your channel by sharing your videos on social media and collaborating with other YouTubers. Collaborating with other creators will help you reach a wider audience, while sharing your videos on social media will make it easier for people to find and watch them.

I am sure that you have got the basic understanding of how YouTube works, how you can make money and what are the steps for creating your own channel. Finally, I would like to give you some useful tips that shall help you during your video creation journey.

1. **Be unique**: One of the best ways to stand out on YouTube is to find a niche or angle for your videos that sets them apart from others in your field. This could be a specific topic, a unique style of filming, or a particular type of humor. By focusing on something that makes your content different, you'll be more likely to attract an audience that is genuinely interested in what you have to say.

2. **Tell a story**: People are more likely to engage with and remember videos that have a clear beginning, middle, and end. Telling a story in your videos can help keep your audience interested and make your content more memorable. This can be done through the use of characters, a narrative arc, or even through the use of visual storytelling techniques.

3. **Use high-quality equipment**: Investing in good camera, microphone, and editing software is crucial for making professional looking videos. High-quality equipment can help make your videos look more polished and increase the chances of your content being shared and

recommended.

4. **Create a consistent look and feel**: Use a consistent color palette, font, and overall aesthetic to create a cohesive brand for your channel. A consistent look and feel will help your viewers identify your videos and channel, and make it easier for them to follow your content.

5. **Use humor**: Humor is a great way to connect with your audience and make your videos more entertaining. Incorporating humor into your content can help make your channel more relatable, increase engagement and make it more memorable.

6. **Collaborating with other YouTubers** can help you reach new audiences and create unique content. Collaborations can also help you learn from other creators and improve your own videos.

7. **Engage with your audience**: Responding to comments and creating a sense of community on your channel by encouraging viewer participation will help build a loyal fan base. Responding to comments and messages can make your audience feel valued and appreciated.

8. **Be authentic and relatable**: Be yourself and don't be afraid to show your personality in your videos. Being authentic and relatable will help create a connection with your audience and make them more likely to continue watching your videos.

9. **Keep it short and sweet**: Attention spans are short, so try to keep your videos under 10 minutes if possible. This will make it more likely for your audience to watch the entire video and help increase engagement.

10. **Experiment and iterate**: Try new things and don't be afraid to make mistakes. Use data and feedback from your audience to improve your content. Experimenting with different types of videos, filming styles, and editing techniques will help you find what works best for your audience and channel.

Cost and Benefit of Being a YouTuber

Being a YouTuber can be a great way to turn your passion for creating content into a career. However, it's important to understand the costs and benefits of starting a YouTube channel before diving in. Here are some key points to consider:

Costs

- **Equipment**: To start a YouTube channel, you will need a camera, a microphone, and editing software. These can be costly, but the prices vary depending on the quality of the equipment.
- **Time**: Creating and uploading videos takes a lot of time and effort. You will need to be prepared to spend a significant amount of time on video production, editing, and promotion.
- **Promotion**: To grow your channel, you will need to promote your videos through social media and other marketing channels. This can also be costly.

Benefits

- **Income**: Successful YouTubers can earn money through advertising revenue, sponsorships, and merchandise sales. The more views and subscribers you have, the more money you can potentially earn.
- **Creative control**: As a YouTuber, you have complete control over the content you create and how you present it.
- **Building a community**: YouTube allows you to connect with like-minded people and build a community around your channel.
- **Flexibility**: You can work from anywhere and on your own schedule.
- **Personal growth**: it's a great way to improve your communication and video making skills

It's important to keep in mind that the costs and benefits of being a YouTuber can vary depending on your niche, audience and the effort you put in. It's not a get rich quick scheme but with patience and hard work, it can be a great way to turn your passion into a career.

Skills Required

Being a successful YouTuber requires a variety of skills, including:

- **Video production**: This includes filming, editing, and post-production. You'll need to be able to create high-quality videos that are visually pleasing and engaging.
- **Writing and storytelling**: Creating a YouTube channel is all about telling stories and providing value to your audience. You'll need to be able to craft compelling and engaging scripts that keep your viewers interested.

- **Marketing and promotion**: You'll need to be able to promote your channel and your videos in order to reach a larger audience. This includes creating social media posts, running ads, and collaborating with other YouTubers.
- **Audience engagement**: Building a community of loyal viewers is crucial for the success of a YouTube channel. You'll need to be able to engage with your audience and build a relationship with them.
- **Technical skills**: Depending on the type of content you create, you may need to have a good understanding of various technical skills, such as video editing software, graphic design, or coding.
- **Creativity**: Above all, to be a successful YouTuber, you need to be creative and unique. You need to create content that stands out from the rest and appeal to the audience.

Call-to-Action

Starting a YouTube channel can seem daunting, especially as a beginner. However, remember that everyone starts somewhere. The most important thing is to just start. Even if your first few videos are not perfect, that's okay. With time and practice, you will improve and develop your own unique style. Remember to be consistent, engage with your audience, and most importantly, have fun. Creating videos should be an enjoyable experience, not a chore. Keep in mind that success on YouTube doesn't happen overnight, it takes time and effort, but with dedication and hard work, you can build a loyal audience who will enjoy and appreciate your content. Don't be afraid to experiment and try new things, who knows, you might just find your niche and create something truly special.

ppp

TWO
STOCK TRADING

Understanding the Trading

Imagine you're sitting at a bar with your friend, and he starts telling you about this amazing thing called stock trading. "Basically," he says, "it's like playing the stock market. You buy shares of a company's stock, and then you can sell them later when the price goes up. It's like buying a piece of that company and making money off of it. It's so cool!" You're intrigued, and ask him to explain more. He goes on to tell you about how he has a trading account with a broker, and he spends his free time analyzing the market and researching different stocks. He tells you about the different types of trading, like day trading and options trading, and how each one has its own set of risks and rewards. You're fascinated by the idea of being able to make money just by buying and selling shares of a company, and you decide to look into it more. And who knows, maybe you'll even start your own trading journey!

As your friend continues to talk about stock trading, you start to ask more questions. You ask him how he got started and he tells you that he started by doing a lot of research and reading books on the subject. He also took a couple of online courses to learn the basics and gain a deeper understanding of the market. He also mentions that he has a mentor who has been guiding him along the way and providing valuable insights.

You ask him about the risks involved and he tells you that stock trading can be risky but also rewarding if done correctly. He also mentions that it's important to have a clear strategy, manage risk and have discipline in order to be successful. He also tells you that it's important to diversify your portfolio and not to put all eggs in one basket.

You also ask him about the returns and he tells you that it varies from person to person, it's not a get-rich-quick scheme but with the right approach and enough time, it can be a good source of income.

You thank your friend for the information and tell him that you're definitely going to look into it more. You're excited by the idea of potentially earning money through stock trading and can't wait to learn more about it.

And you jokingly add "I hope I don't end up like those meme traders who bought Satyam Computer shares" and both of you laugh.

Welcome to the world of stock trading, where the potential for high returns and financial freedom awaits those who are willing to take on the risk and put in the work. It's a fast-paced and dynamic world where one can make money by buying and selling shares of a company. However, it's important to note that it's not just about buying low and selling high, it's about having a clear strategy, conducting thorough research, monitoring the market and managing risk. It's a world where discipline, patience and the ability to adapt are key to success. The world of stock trading can be intimidating, especially for beginners, but with the right mindset, tools, and guidance, anyone can learn to navigate it and potentially reap the rewards.

Why Should You Trade in Stock Market?

Alright, so you're thinking about getting into stock trading. You've heard it can be a pretty sweet deal, but you're probably wondering what's in it for you. Well, let me break it down for you.

First of all, there's the potential for some serious cash. If you play your cards right and make smart trades, you can make a pretty penny off your investments. Let's say you invested in a company like Reliance Industries, a blue-chip company in India, a few years ago. If you held on to your shares, you would have seen a significant return on your investment as the company's stock price has risen over time. Yeah, there's always the chance of losing money too, but that's true with any kind of investing. The key is to manage your risk and not invest more than you can afford to lose.

Another cool thing about stock trading is that you're in the driver's seat. Unlike some other types of investing, like mutual funds, you get to choose what stocks you buy and sell. This means you can tailor your portfolio to your own interests and risk tolerance. Plus, you're not just relying on some fund manager to make decisions for you.

Stock trading can also be pretty flexible. Sure, you'll need to keep an eye on the market, but you can do that from anywhere with an internet connection. Plus, you can trade on your own schedule. Whether you're a stay-at-home parent, a student, or just someone with a 9-5 job, you can trade stocks around your other commitments. If you're a busy person with a full-time job but want to make your own investment decisions, stock trading is a great option. You can use online trading platforms like Zerodha, Upstox, or ICICI Direct to make trades on your own schedule.

But, perhaps the most exciting reason to consider stock trading is that it can be a lot of fun! There's something thrilling about making a trade and watching the stock price go up. It's like a game, and who doesn't love a good game? Plus, there's a sense of accomplishment that comes with making a smart trade. It's like solving a puzzle, and when it pays off, it's pretty satisfying.

Another benefit of stock trading is diversification. By investing in different types of stocks, from different industries, and with different levels of risk, you can spread out the risk and maximize your returns. And if you're feeling fancy, you can even use leverage to amplify your potential returns. Instead of putting all your eggs in one basket and investing in just one company, you can diversify your portfolio by investing in a variety of different companies across different sectors. For example, you can invest in the IT sector by buying shares of TATA Consultancy Services (TCS), in the banking sector by buying shares of HDFC Bank, in the FMCG sector by buying shares of HUL. This can help you to spread out risk and maximize returns.

And let's not forget about liquidity. Stocks are considered liquid assets, meaning they can be easily bought or sold in a short period of time. This allows you to quickly react to market changes and make trades. For example, if you see a sudden drop in the value of a stock, you can sell it off quickly, to minimize your losses. Plus, some stocks even pay dividends, which means you can earn some passive income. For example, a company like Tata Steel, pays dividends to its shareholders, providing a source of passive income.

But, before you jump in headfirst, keep in mind that stock trading isn't a get-rich-quick scheme. It takes time, effort, and a solid understanding of the market to be successful. But, if you're ready to put in the work and have a little bit of fun, stock trading might just be the perfect fit for you. And if you get really good at it, you might even be able to afford that fancy car you've been dreaming of, or even a private island (but let's not get ahead of ourselves here, one step at a time!)

Step-by-Step Guide

Trading in the stock market can be a great way to make money, but it's important to be informed and have a strategy in place. The Indian stock market, also known as the National Stock Exchange (NSE) and the Bombay Stock Exchange (BSE), offers a wide range of opportunities for traders of all levels. In this guide, we'll go over the steps you need to take to start trading in the Indian stock market.

1. **Research and educate yourself**: Before you start trading, it's important to learn about the stock market, how it works and the different types of stocks you can invest in. You can do this by reading books, taking online courses, or even finding a mentor.
2. **Open a trading account**: In order to buy and sell stocks, you'll need to open a trading account with a broker. There are many online brokers in India like Zerodha, Upstox, ICICI Direct and many more.
3. **Fund your account**: Once you have your trading account set up, you'll need to fund it. This can typically be done through online transfer, cheques, or even cash deposits.
4. **Choose a stock**: With your trading account set up and funded, you can start looking for stocks to invest in. Be sure to conduct thorough research and due diligence on any stock before you invest.
5. **Place an order**: Once you've found a stock you're interested in, you can place an order to buy or sell shares. This can typically be done through your trading account.
6. **Monitor your investments**: After you've made your trades, it's important to monitor your investments and stay up-to-date on the market trends.
7. **Exit strategy**: It's always important to have an exit strategy before entering a trade, whether it's a stop-loss or a profit target.
8. **Evaluate your performance**: Keep track of your performance, and evaluate your trades regularly. This will help you to identify your strengths and weaknesses and make adjustments accordingly.

It's important to remember that stock trading carries risk and it's important to have a clear understanding of the market and have a strategy to manage risk. It's also important to remember that past performance is not an indicator of future performance, so it's essential to do your own research and invest in companies that align with your goals and risk tolerance. It's also important to consult with a financial advisor before making any investment decisions.

It's also important to remember that stock trading requires patience and discipline, you should never chase the trend and follow a long-term plan rather than short-term gains. It's also important to keep an eye on the global market and the news that might affect the Indian market.

In summary, stock trading can be a great way to make money, but it's important to be informed, have a strategy and manage risk. With the right approach, patience, and a bit of luck, you can make some good money and have fun doing it.

Skills Required

If you're thinking about getting into stock trading, there are a few key skills you'll need to develop in order to be a consistent, profitable trader. Here is an example of a conversation between you and a friend who is also a trader.

- **You**: "Hey, I've been thinking about getting into stock trading, but I'm not sure if I have what it takes. What do you think?"
- **Friend**: "Well, it definitely takes some work to become a consistent, profitable trader. But, if you're willing to put in the effort, I think you can do it."
- **You**: "Yeah, I'm willing to put in the work. But, what kind of skills do I need to have?"
- **Friend**: "First and foremost, you need to have a solid understanding of the market. This means keeping up with market trends, economic news, and company earnings. You'll also need to know how to conduct thorough research and due diligence on potential stocks to invest in."
- **You**: "Got it. What else?"
- **Friend**: "Risk management is key. Trading stocks carries risk, and it's important to have a clear understanding of your risk tolerance and to have a strategy in place to manage that risk. Patience and discipline are also crucial. You need to have a long-term plan and not to chase short-term gains. It's also important to not get too caught up in the emotions of the market, and to stick to your plan even when things get tough."

- **You**: "Wow, that sounds like a lot to handle."
- **Friend**: "It can be, but it's definitely doable. And don't forget, being able to make quick decisions, based on your research and analysis will give you an edge over other traders, and it's important to evaluate your performance and learn from your mistakes."
- **You**: "Okay, that sounds more manageable. Thanks for the advice, I think I'm ready to give it a try."
- **Friend**: "Of course, I'm happy to help. Just remember, it takes time and effort to become a successful trader, but with the right approach, you can do it."
- **You**: "Yeah, I'm ready to put in the work. But, where should I start?"
- **Friend**: "The first step is to open a trading account with a broker. There are many online brokers in India like Zerodha, Upstox, ICICI Direct and many more. Once you have your account set up, you'll need to fund it, and you can start researching stocks to invest in."
- **You**: "Okay, I'll look into that. But, what should I be looking for in a stock?"
- **Friend**: "It depends on your goals and risk tolerance. But, generally, you'll want to look for companies with strong financials, a solid track record, and a promising future outlook. You should also consider the industry and sector the company operates in and the overall market conditions."
- **You**: "Got it, thanks. I'll start doing my research."
- **Friend**: "Sounds good. Remember, the key to success in stock trading is to be informed, have a strategy, and manage risk. And always be prepared to make quick decisions based on your research and analysis."
- **You**: "I'll keep that in mind. Thanks for all the help, I feel much more confident now."
- **Friend**: "No problem, happy to help. And remember, if you have any questions or need any advice, don't hesitate to reach out."
- **You**: "Got it, I'll keep you updated on my progress. Maybe one day I'll be the next Rakesh Jhunjhunwala"
- **Friend**: "Ha! I wouldn't hold your breath for that, but who knows, you might just surprise us all!"

In the above conversation, the two individuals discussed the necessary skills required for consistent profitability in stock trading within the Indian market. They emphasized the importance of market understanding, comprehensive research, effective risk management, discipline, patience, prompt decision making, performance evaluation and continuous learning. Additionally, they discussed the initial steps for initiating stock trading, including opening a trading account with a broker and conducting research on potential stocks to invest in. The conversation emphasized that the key to success in stock trading is to maintain an informed perspective, have a well-defined strategy, and effectively manage risk.

Cost and Benefit

Making a monthly income through trading can be a great way to supplement your income, but it's important to weigh the costs and benefits before diving in.

One of the biggest benefits of trading is the potential to make a significant income in a short amount of time. If you're skilled and disciplined, you could potentially make hundreds or even thousands of dollars a day. This can be a great way to reach financial goals or achieve financial freedom.

However, it's important to keep in mind that trading is a high-risk strategy, and there is a potential to lose money as well as make it. It's crucial to have a well-defined strategy, manage risk and have realistic expectations when it comes to earning potential. Trading requires a lot of discipline, and it's important to be able to make quick decisions based on your research and analysis.

The cost of trading can include the need for a significant amount of capital, and the cost of a trading account and education. It's also important to consider the time and effort required to stay informed and up-to-date on market trends, company earnings and global news.

In summary, making a monthly income through trading can be a great way to supplement your income, but it's important to weigh the costs and benefits before diving in. Trading is a high-risk strategy, but with the right approach, discipline and knowledge, it can be a powerful tool to gain control over your financial future and achieve your dreams.

Call-to-Action

Stock trading can be a great way to take control of your financial future and achieve your financial goals. It may seem daunting at first, but with the right mindset and approach, anyone can learn the basics and start making money through stock trading. It takes discipline, patience, and a willingness to learn and adapt, but with hard work and dedication, you can become a successful trader. The earning potential is significant and it could be a powerful tool to reach your financial goals, whether it be paying off debt, saving for a down payment on a house, or achieving financial freedom. Remember, the stock market is a marathon and not a sprint, so don't be afraid to make mistakes, learn from them and keep moving forward. With the right mindset, anything is possible.

Stock trading is not just about making money, it's also about learning about the markets and the economy, and taking an active role in managing your financial future. It's a journey of continuous learning and growth, and the more you learn, the better you'll become. With the right approach, you can learn to think like a trader, develop a winning strategy and become a master of risk management. The best part is that you don't have to have a lot of money to start trading stocks, you can start small and work your way up as you gain more knowledge and experience.

Additionally, it's also important to remember that stock trading is not a get-rich-quick scheme, it takes time, effort, and a solid understanding of the market to be successful. It's important to have realistic expectations and not to be discouraged if you experience losses in the beginning. Every successful trader has gone through their fair share of losses, but they've learned from their mistakes and kept moving forward.

So, if you're ready to take control of your financial future and achieve your financial goals, stock trading may be the perfect fit for you. With the right mindset, approach, and dedication, you can become a successful trader and reach your financial goals.

If you're ready to take control of your financial future and achieve your financial goals, stock trading may be the perfect fit for you. With the right mindset, approach, and dedication, you can become a successful trader and reach your financial goals. Just remember, if at first you don't succeed in the stock market, try, try again. Who knows, you might just be the next Rakesh Jhunjhunwala or Warren Buffett of the stock market world!!!

ᢣᢣᢣ

THREE

CREATING ONLINE COURSE

Once upon a time, there was a person named Jack who was an expert in gardening. Jack had been gardening for years and had accumulated a wealth of knowledge and experience. He loved gardening so much that he wanted to share his knowledge with others. One day, Jack had an idea. He thought, "Why not create an online course about gardening and share my knowledge with people all over the world?" So, he got to work.

First, he had to decide on a structure for the course. He broke it down into different sections, such as basics of gardening, how to choose the right soil, how to plant, how to maintain, how to harvest and how to deal with pests and diseases.

Next, he had to create content for the course. He created videos, wrote articles, and made presentations. He also included pictures and diagrams to make the course more interactive and easy to understand.

Once the content was ready, he had to decide on a platform to host the course. He chose a popular online learning platform, like Udemy, which allowed him to create a course, put it online and make it accessible to a wide audience.

Finally, he launched the course and started promoting it. He shared it on social media, reached out to gardening clubs and groups and even put up posters in his local area.

To his surprise, the course was a huge success! People from all over the world enrolled and left positive reviews. Jack was thrilled that he was able to share his passion and knowledge with others and help them learn more about gardening.

From that day on, Jack became known as the "Gardening Guru" and his online course became one of the most popular gardening courses on the internet. He even started making money from it! He was able to turn his passion into a business and help others at the same time. The prospect of developing an online course might appear intimidating, but as Jack's story shows, it's a great way to share your knowledge and experience with others, and even turn it into a business opportunity.

In conclusion, Jack's story is a testament to the power of turning one's passion into a business opportunity. He saw a need for people to learn more about gardening, and created an online course to meet that need. His hard work and dedication paid off, as the course was a huge success, and he was able to share his knowledge and passion with people all over the world. This not only helped him make money but also helped him to connect with like-minded people who shared his passion. His story shows that if you have a passion, and the willingness to put in the work, you can turn it into a successful business. And that's what makes the story of Jack a true inspiration.

Just like Jack, you too can turn your passion into a business opportunity by creating an online course. It may seem challenging, but with hard work and dedication, you can share your knowledge and experience with people all over the world. You don't need to be a "guru" in a field, you just need to have a passion for something and be willing to put in the work to make it happen. Look at Jack's story, he started as a passionate gardener and ended up becoming the "Gardening Guru" and making money from it. It's not just about making money, it's also about making a difference and connecting with like-minded people who share your passion. So, don't wait any longer, take the first step and start creating your online course today. Who knows, you might just become the next "Gardening Guru" or "Cooking Queen" or "Fitness King" and make money while doing something you love.

Why Should You Consider Creating Online Course?

Creating an online course is a great way to share your knowledge and experience with others while turning your passion into a business opportunity.

First of all, let's talk about the reach of your online course. When you create an online course, you are not limited to a specific location or a certain group of people. An online course can be accessed by anyone, anywhere, at any time. This means that you can reach a much wider audience than if you were to teach in person. For example, if you're an expert in gardening and you want to share your knowledge with others, you can create an online course and reach people all over the world who are interested in gardening.

Another benefit of creating an online course is the flexibility it offers. You can create and promote your course whenever you want. You don't have to be tied to a specific schedule or location. For example, if you're a stay-at-home mom who wants to share your cooking skills, you can create an online course and promote it during your free time, like when your kids are in school.

Sharing your expertise is another great benefit of creating an online course. When you create an online course, you have the opportunity to share your knowledge and experience with others. It's a great way to help others and make a difference. For example, if you're an expert in photography, you can create an online course and teach people how to take better pictures.

Making money is another great benefit of creating an online course. You can sell access to your course, or even create a membership site and charge a monthly or annual fee. For example, if you're a graphic designer, you can create an online course on graphic design and charge people to access it.

Last but not least, creating an online course allows you to learn and grow as a professional. You will have to research and prepare content, which will help you learn more about your field. Additionally, by interacting with students, you will gain new perspective and insights. For example, if you're a fitness trainer, you can create an online course and learn more about the latest fitness trends and techniques by interacting with your students.

In conclusion, creating an online course is a great way to share your knowledge and experience with others, turn your passion into a business opportunity, and make money while doing something you love and also develop your skills and knowledge further. Whether you're an expert in gardening, cooking, photography, graphic design, or fitness, creating an online course can help you share your passion with others, make a difference, and even make a living doing something you love. So, don't let your knowledge and experience go to waste, consider creating an online course and see where it takes you. Remember, the possibilities are endless, you just need to take the first step and start creating your online course today.

There are many success stories of people who have created and profited from online courses. Here are a few examples:

1. **Jon Morrow** is an entrepreneur who created an online course called "Blog Launch" which teaches people how to start a successful blog. He has sold over $1 million worth of this course and has helped thousands of people start their own blogs.
2. **Ramit Sethi**, a personal finance expert, has helped thousands of people increase their income with his online course "Earn 1K," which has generated over $12 million in sales.
3. **Pat Flynn** is an online entrepreneur who created an online course called "Smart from Scratch" which teaches people how to start an online business from scratch. He has sold over $1 million worth of this course and has helped thousands of people start their own online businesses.
4. **Neil Patel** is a digital marketing expert who created an online course called "Advanced Marketing Program" which teaches people how to grow their business through digital marketing. He has sold over $10 million worth of this course and has helped thousands of people grow their business online.
5. **Rosie King** is a mental health advocate who created an online course called "The Self-Care Solution" which teaches people how to take care of their mental health. She has sold over $1 million worth of this course and has helped thousands of people improve their mental health.
6. **Sandeep Maheshwari** is an Indian entrepreneur and motivational speaker who created an online course called "Unlimited Power" which teaches people how to achieve success and live their best lives. He has sold over $10 million worth of this course and has helped thousands of people in India achieve their goals.
7. **Meera Kaul** is an Indian businesswoman and entrepreneur who created an online course called "Mastering Business" which teaches people how to start and grow a successful business. She has sold over $1 million worth of this course and has helped thousands of Indian entrepreneurs start and grow their own businesses.
8. **Deepak Kanakaraju** is an Indian digital marketing expert who created an online course called "Digital Marketing Mastery" which teaches people how to grow their business through digital marketing. He has sold over $5 million worth of this course and has helped thousands of Indian businesses grow their online presence.

9. **Prasanna Chandra** is an Indian financial expert who created an online course called "Investment Mastery" which teaches people how to invest in the stock market and make money. He has sold over $2 million worth of this course and has helped thousands of Indian people invest in the stock market and make money.

10. **Suhasini Verma** is an Indian teacher who created an online course called "Mastering English" which teaches people how to improve their English language skills. She has sold over $1 million worth of this course and has helped thousands of Indian people improve their English language skills.

These are just a few examples, but there are thousands of other people who have created and profited from online courses. According to a recent report, the global e-learning market size is expected to reach $325 billion by 2025. This shows that creating an online course can be a lucrative business and it's a great way to share your knowledge and experience with others.

Creating an online course can be a great way to share your knowledge and experience with others while turning your passion into a business opportunity. Just look at the success stories of people like Jon Morrow, Ramit Sethi, Pat Flynn, Neil Patel, Rosie King, Sandeep Maheshwari, Meera Kaul, Deepak Kanakaraju, Prasanna Chandra, and Suhasini Verma. They all created successful online courses and profited from them. They all have different background, expertise and niches but they all have one thing in common, they are successful in creating and profiting from online courses. Each one of them has helped thousands of people learn new skills and reach their goals, and they have also been able to make a living doing something they love. If they can do it, so can you. You have the knowledge and experience, you just need to take the first step and start creating your online course today.

Step-by-Step Guide

Well before we learn the guide to create your online course and make money, lets see the areas in which couses can be made.

1. Cooking
2. Programming
3. Stock trading
4. Yoga

5. Photography
6. Personal development
7. Business management
8. Graphic design
9. Fitness
10. Language learning
11. Music production
12. Digital marketing
13. Painting
14. Writing
15. Personal finance
16. Home renovation
17. Web development
18. Fashion design
19. Medical coding
20. Project management
21. Interior design
22. Game development
23. SEO
24. Yoga teacher training
25. Film production
26. Event planning
27. Personal styling
28. Home schooling
29. Pet grooming
30. Make-up artistry
31. Gardening

This list is not exhaustive, as there are many more areas in which online courses can be made, depending on the creator's expertise and interests.

Creating an online course can be a great way to share your knowledge and experience with others, and even turn it into a business opportunity. Here are the general steps to create an online course:

- **Identify your niche**: Determine what you are passionate about and what you are an expert in. For example, if you are a professional chef and have experience in Indian cuisine, then you can create a course that teaches people how to cook Indian food. If you are a software developer with experience in a specific programming language, then you can create a course that teaches people how to code in that language.

- **Define your course content**: Break down your course into different sections or modules. For example, if you are creating a course on Indian cuisine, you can divide it into sections on appetizers, main course, and dessert. If you are creating a course on coding, you can divide it into sections on basic concepts, data structures, and algorithms.
- **Create your course content**: Use a variety of media such as videos, audio, PDFs, and images to create engaging and interactive content. For example, if you are creating a course on Indian cuisine, you can create videos of you cooking different dishes and provide the recipes in PDF format. If you are creating a course on coding, you can create videos that explain different concepts and provide examples and exercises in the form of PDFs or images.
- **Choose a platform**: Decide on a platform to host your course. Popular options include Udemy, Coursera, Thinkific, Teachable and many more. Each platform has its own set of features, pricing, and audience. For example, if your course is focused on a specific niche, you might want to choose a platform that caters to that niche.
- **Promote your course**: Use social media, email marketing, and other channels to promote your course and attract students. For example, you can create a website, use social media platforms like Facebook, Twitter, Instagram, and LinkedIn to promote your course, and reach out to influencers in your niche to promote your course.
- **Monitor and evaluate**: Keep track of your student's progress and gather feedback to improve your course content and delivery. For example, you can use analytics tools to track the progress of your students, gather feedback through surveys and use it to improve your course.
- **Monetize your course**: Decide on a pricing strategy and monetize your course by charging for access or offering a subscription service. For example, you can charge a one-time fee for access to your course or you can offer a subscription service where students can access all your courses for a monthly or annual fee.

Please note that this is a general guide and each platform or course may have different requirements, so make sure to read and understand them before creating your course.

There are several platforms available to host your online course, here are few popular ones:

- **Udemy**: A widely used platform that offers a wide range of courses and allows you to reach a large audience.
- **Coursera**: A platform that partners with universities and organizations to offer online courses.
- **Teachable**:The platform provides you with multiple customization options to create, market, and sell your course.
- **Skillshare**: A platform that focuses on creative and design courses, and offers a subscription-based model.
- **Ruzuku**: A platform that allows you to create and sell online courses, with a focus on simplicity and ease of use.
- **LearnWorlds**: A platform that allows you to create and sell online courses, with a focus on interactive and multimedia content.
- **OpenSesame**: A platform that allows you to access and purchase online courses from a variety of providers.

These are just a few examples of the many platforms available, and each has its own set of features and pricing plans. It's important to research and compare different platforms to find the one that best suits your needs.

Udemy is the most popular online learning and teaching platform that provides a wide range of courses on various topics such as business, technology, personal development, and more. The platform was founded in 2010 and is headquartered in San Francisco, California. Udemy has more than 130,000 courses and 35 million students worldwide and is available in more than 50 languages. It is a popular choice among students and instructors alike as it offers flexibility, affordability, and access to a wide range of content.

Suppose you want to create a course where you teach about gardening. Creating an online course on Udemy using gardening as an example is a great way to share your knowledge and experience with others, and even turn it into a business opportunity. Here are the steps to create an online course on Udemy:

- **Sign up for Udemy**: Go to the Udemy website and create an account.
- **Create your course**: Click on the "Teach on Udemy" button and start creating your course. You will be prompted to give your course a title, a

subtitle, and a short description.

- **Define the course content**: Break down your course into different sections or modules. For example, if you are creating a course on gardening, you can divide it into sections on basics of gardening, how to choose the right soil, how to plant, how to maintain, how to harvest and how to deal with pests and diseases.
- **Create your course content**: Use a variety of media such as videos, audio, PDFs, and images to create engaging and interactive content. For example, you can create videos of you gardening different plants and provide the instructions in PDF format.
- **Record your videos**: Record your videos using a camera or a screen recording software. Make sure the videos are of good quality, well-lit and easy to understand.
- **Add the course content**: Once you have recorded your videos, add them to the course sections you created earlier. You can also add any additional materials like PDFs, images or quizzes to the course.
- **Set a price for the course**: Decide on a pricing strategy and set a price for your course. Udemy allows you to set a price or offer a free course. You can set a price for your course and Udemy will take a commission on each sale. The amount of commission varies depending on the price of the course and your country of residence, but it typically ranges from 25% to 50%.
- **Publish your course**: Once you have completed all the above steps, you can publish your course and make it available to the public.
- **Promote your course**: Share your course on social media, reach out to gardening clubs and groups and even put up posters in your local area to attract more students.
- **Monitor and evaluate**: Keep track of your student's progress and gather feedback to improve your course content and delivery.

Please note that this is a general guide and each platform or course may have different requirements, so make sure to read and understand them before creating your course.

By creating a course on Udemy, you can reach a global audience and share your expertise with students from all over the world. Udemy is a well-established and reputable platform, with a large student base, which can increase your visibility and credibility as an expert in your field.

Additionally, creating a course on Udemy is relatively simple and straightforward, with a user-friendly interface, and provides you with all the tools and resources you need to create, market and sell your course. Udemy also allows you to set your own prices and offer discounts, which can be a great way to attract more students and increase your earning potential.

Furthermore, Udemy also provides you with valuable analytics and insights, which can help you understand how your course is performing and how you can improve it. Additionally, Udemy also has an affiliate program, which can help you earn extra income by promoting other instructors' courses.

In summary, creating and selling a course on Udemy can be a great way to turn your passion and expertise into a profitable business, while also reaching a global audience and helping others learn new skills and improve their careers.

Cost and Benefit of Creating Online Course

Creating an online course is a great way to share your knowledge and expertise with others and earn money while doing it. However, before you jump in and start creating your course, it's important to understand that it does come with its own set of costs.

First and foremost, creating an online course requires a significant amount of time and effort. You'll need to research your topic, create content, and promote your course. This can be a time-consuming process, and it's important to be prepared to invest the necessary time and effort to create a high-quality course.

In addition to time and effort, creating an online course also requires some equipment. A computer, camera, and other equipment may be needed to create your course content. This can be an additional cost to consider when creating an online course.

Another cost to consider is the platform fee. Some platforms like Udemy charge a fee to host your course, which is something to keep in mind when choosing a platform to host your course.

Despite these costs, the benefits of creating an online course can be substantial. One of the biggest benefits is the potential for passive income. Once your course is created, it can continue to generate income for you, even when you're not actively working on it. This means that the time and effort you put in upfront can pay off in the long term.

Another benefit of creating an online course is the ability to reach a global audience. With an online course, you can share your knowledge and expertise with students from all over the world, which can be a great way to expand your reach and impact.

Creating an online course also allows you to share your knowledge and experience with others, which can be incredibly rewarding. By helping others learn new skills and improve their careers, you can make a real difference in the lives of others.

Furthermore, creating an online course gives you the flexibility to work from anywhere, at any time. This can be a great way to balance work and personal life and allows you to work on your own terms.

In summary, creating an online course can be a great way to monetize your knowledge and skills, and make a difference in the lives of others. However, it's important to be aware of the costs involved and be prepared to invest the necessary time and effort to create a high-quality course. Despite the costs, the potential benefits of creating an online course can be well worth it in the long run.

Skills Required

Creating an online course requires a variety of skills, and acquiring those skills can be done in a variety of ways. Some of the most important skills include:

- **Subject matter expertise**: To create an effective online course, you must have a deep understanding of the topic you are teaching. If you don't have expertise in a certain subject, you can acquire it by researching and studying the topic, or by taking courses or earning certifications in that field.
- **Content creation**: To create an online course, you'll need to be able to create high-quality content that is easy to understand and engaging for your students. This can include creating videos, writing articles, and creating presentations. You can take courses on video and content creation, or practice creating content on your own.
- **Technical skills**: Creating an online course requires a variety of technical skills, such as using video editing software, creating and editing images, and using course platforms. There are a variety of free tutorials on YouTube that teach these skills for free.

- **Promotion and marketing**: To make your course successful, you'll need to be able to effectively promote and market it. This includes creating a landing page, creating marketing materials, and using social media to drive traffic to your course.
- **Teaching and instruction**: Creating an online course requires you to have the ability to teach and instruct others.

Acquiring these skills can take time and effort, but it's important to remember that you don't need to be an expert in every area. You can always outsource certain aspects of course creation, such as editing or marketing, if you feel more comfortable doing so. The key is to be aware of the skills required to create an online course and take the necessary steps to acquire them.

When creating an online course, there are several tips to keep in mind to ensure its success:

- **Start with a clear goal**: Before creating your course, it's important to have a clear idea of what you want to achieve. This can include the specific skills or knowledge you want to impart to your students, as well as the outcome you want them to achieve.
- **Make it interactive**: To keep your students engaged and motivated, it's important to make your course as interactive as possible. This can include incorporating quizzes, discussions, and hands-on activities throughout the course.
- **Use a variety of media**: To keep your students engaged and to cater to different learning styles, it's important to use a variety of media in your course. This can include videos, images, audio, and written content.
- **Keep it organized**: It's important to keep your course organized and easy to navigate. This can include using clear headings and subheadings, and providing a clear outline of the course's structure.
- **Provide feedback and support**: To ensure your students are getting the most out of your course, it's important to provide them with feedback and support throughout the course. This can include answering questions, providing additional resources, and creating a community where students can support and learn from one another.
- **Have a plan for promotion**: Creating a course is just one step, the other most important step is to promote it to the right audience, this could be done through social media marketing, email marketing, content

marketing, and paid advertising.

- **Continuously improve**: Once you've launched your course, it's important to continuously improve it based on student feedback and engagement. This can include updating content, adding new features, and addressing any issues that arise.

By following these tips, you can create an online course that is engaging, informative, and effective for your students.

Call-to-Action

So, are you ready to take the plunge and create your own online course? Don't let fear or uncertainty hold you back! Remember, the skills and knowledge you have are valuable and in demand, and creating an online course is a great way to share them with others and earn money while doing it.

Start by setting a clear goal for your course and mapping out the content you want to cover. Then, take the time to acquire the necessary skills, whether it be through taking courses or learning on your own. And don't forget to have fun with it! Creating an online course is an exciting and rewarding journey.

Just remember, the best time to start was yesterday, the next best time is now! So, go ahead and start creating your course today, you'll be glad you did! So, don't wait any longer to share your wisdom with the world and make some extra cash on the side. Just think, you could be the next online course sensation, like the "Gardening Guru" or the "Stock Trading Pro"! And who knows, you might even be able to retire early and finally have the time to do all the things you've always wanted to do, like gardening or trading... or even just sleeping in!

ᚦᚦᚦ

FOUR
SELLING ONLINE COURSE

Have you ever thought about how you could make money by selling online courses created by other people? It may seem like a strange concept, but it's actually a pretty simple and profitable way to earn some extra cash. Here are a few thought-provoking questions to consider:

- Have you ever come across a course that you thought was really valuable, but didn't have the time or money to take it yourself?
- Have you ever wished there was a way to share that course with others and earn a commission for it?
- Have you ever heard of affiliate marketing, where you earn a commission for promoting someone else's product?

Well, you're in luck, because all of these scenarios are possible when it comes to selling online courses created by other people. In fact, it's a great way to earn money without having to create a course yourself. All you need to do is find a course that you believe in, promote it to others, and earn a commission for every sale that you make.

So, are you ready to start earning money by selling online courses of other creators? It's a great way to make some extra cash and help others learn new skills at the same time. And who knows, maybe you'll even discover a new passion for teaching and learning. Just remember, as with any business, it takes time and effort to build up a successful course-selling empire. But, if you're up for the challenge, the rewards can be pretty sweet. And if you're not, well, at least you'll have a good excuse to procrastinate and watch cat videos on YouTube instead. So, you can start your journey of selling the online course today!

Why Sell Online Courses?

Selling online courses of other creators is a great way to make money in today's digital age. With the rise of the internet and mobile technology, more and more people are turning to online education to learn new skills and advance their careers. And as a result, the market for online courses has exploded in recent years.

One of the biggest reasons why selling online courses has gained momentum is that it offers a low-risk, high-reward business model. Unlike traditional brick-and-mortar businesses, you don't need to invest a lot of money upfront to get started. All you need is a computer and internet connection, and you can be up and running in no time. Plus, since you're not creating the course content yourself, you don't have to worry about spending countless hours researching, writing, and editing. Instead, you can focus on promoting and selling the course.

Another reason why selling online courses has become so popular is that it offers a great deal of flexibility. You can work from anywhere, at any time, and on your own schedule. This means that you can run your business while still being able to take care of your family, travel, or pursue other interests.

Additionally, selling online courses can be a scalable business. Once you have a course up and running, you can continue to promote and sell it, earning passive income for months or even years to come. This means that with each course you sell, your income has the potential to grow exponentially.

Another benefit of selling online courses is that it allows you to tap into a global market. With the internet, you can reach people from all over the world, which means that you have the potential to earn money from anywhere.

Lastly, selling online courses is a great way to make a difference in people's lives. By offering valuable information and skills, you're helping people to improve their lives and achieve their goals. And that's a pretty amazing feeling.

So, if you're looking for a low-risk, high-reward business model that offers flexibility, scalability, and the potential to make a difference, then selling online courses of other creators might just be the perfect fit for you.

Step-by-Step Guide

In today's digital age, selling courses online has become an increasingly popular way for entrepreneurs, educators, and subject matter experts to share their knowledge and monetize their expertise. Whether you're an experienced teacher or just starting out, the process of creating and selling online courses can be a lucrative way to build a following, share your passion, and generate income.

In this guide, we will walk you through a step-by-step process to help you successfully sell your courses online. From developing your course content to choosing the right platform to marketing and selling your course, we will provide you with practical tips and tools to create and sell your course with confidence. So, let's get started!

- **Researching Potential Courses:**

  - **Identifying profitable niches and in-demand courses**: One of the first things you should do when researching potential courses to sell is to identify profitable niches and in-demand courses. For example, if you're interested in the health and wellness niche, you may want to look for courses related to nutrition, fitness, or mental health. By identifying profitable niches and in-demand courses, you'll be able to target a specific audience and increase your chances of success.
  - **Finding reputable course creators and evaluating their courses**: Once you've identified potential niches and courses, the next step is to find reputable course creators and evaluate their courses. This means looking at the quality of the content, the instructor's qualifications and experience, and the overall value of the course. For example, you can check out the reviews and ratings of the course on the platform it's being sold, and also check out the instructor's profile and qualifications. By finding reputable course creators and evaluating their courses, you'll be able to ensure that you're offering high-quality courses to your audience.

- **Setting Up Your Platform**

- **Choosing a platform to host and sell the courses**: When it comes to setting up your platform to sell online courses: there are a few key things to consider. First and foremost, you need to choose a platform that will best serve your needs. There are a number of different options available, including popular e-commerce platforms like Shopify or WooCommerce, or specialized course hosting platforms like Teachable or Thinkific. For example, if you're looking to sell a wide variety of courses from different creators, an e-commerce platform like Shopify might be the best choice. This platform allows you to easily create an online store, add products, and process payments. On the other hand, if you're only planning to sell courses from one or two creators, a specialized course hosting platform like Teachable might be a better fit. These platforms are designed specifically for hosting and selling online courses, and often come with built-in marketing tools and analytics.

- **Setting up your website or online store:** Once you've chosen a platform, it's time to set up your website or online store. This typically involves creating an account, choosing a template or design, and adding all the necessary information, such as your business name, contact details, and payment options. You'll also need to add your courses and any relevant information, such as course descriptions, pricing, and any discounts or promotions you're offering.

  For example, if you're using Shopify, you can create an account, choose a template and customize it according to your brand and preferences, add all the details, create a course section and add all the courses with their details, pricing, and any discounts and promotions.

  It's important to remember that setting up your platform is an ongoing process. As you start selling courses, you'll want to keep an eye on analytics and make changes as necessary to optimize your sales and customer experience. But with the right platform and a little bit of work, you'll be able to start selling online courses in no time.

- **Marketing and Promoting Your Courses:** When it comes to selling online courses of other creators, marketing and promotion is key.

- **Developing a marketing strategy**: Without a strong marketing strategy, it can be difficult to attract customers and generate sales. So, how do you go about promoting your courses? First, it's important to determine your target audience. Who are the people who are most likely to be interested in the courses you're offering? Once you know your target audience, you can start developing a marketing strategy that will resonate with them.

- **Utilizing social media and other online channels to promote your courses:** One great way to reach your target audience is through social media. Platforms like Facebook, Instagram, and Twitter allow you to connect with potential customers and promote your courses directly to them. You can also use paid advertising options like Facebook ads and Google ads to reach an even wider audience.

  Another effective way to promote your courses is through email marketing. By building a list of email subscribers, you can send out regular updates and promotions directly to people who are interested in your courses.

  Finally, don't underestimate the power of word of mouth. Encourage satisfied customers to spread the word about your courses to their friends and family.

  The key to successfully promoting and marketing your courses is to be creative and think outside the box. By using a combination of these strategies, you'll be able to reach your target audience and generate sales for the online courses you're offering.

- **Earning Revenue:** When it comes to earning revenue from selling online courses, there are a few key things to keep in mind.

- **Setting prices for the courses**: First, you'll need to set prices for the courses you're offering. This can be a tricky task, as you'll need to consider both the value of the course and what similar courses are priced at. One way to do this is to conduct market research and see what other course sellers are charging for similar content.

- **Collecting payments and distributing them to the course creators**: Once you've set prices for your courses, you'll need to figure out how to collect payments from your customers. This typically involves setting up a payment gateway on your website or online store, and there are a variety of options to choose from. PayPal and Stripe are two popular options, and they both offer easy integration with most e-commerce platforms.

Once you've collected payments, it's important to distribute them to the course creators in a timely and efficient manner. This typically involves setting up a system for tracking sales and paying commissions to the creators. Some popular tools for this include Gumroad, which allows you to sell digital products and automatically pay out commissions to creators, and Teachable, which is a platform specifically designed for hosting and selling online courses.

Overall, selling online courses can be a great way to earn money, but it's important to do your research and set up your platform and marketing strategy carefully. By choosing the right courses, setting fair prices, and promoting your offerings effectively, you can build a successful business selling online courses of other creators.

In short, selling online courses of other creators can be a profitable business opportunity. The first step is to research potential courses by identifying profitable niches and in-demand courses, and finding reputable course creators to evaluate. Next, you need to set up your platform by choosing a hosting platform that best suits your needs, and setting up your website or online store. Marketing and promotion is crucial in order to attract customers and generate sales. This can be achieved by developing a marketing strategy that targets your specific audience, and utilizing social media and other online channels to promote your courses. It's important to keep in mind that setting up and running this business is an ongoing process, and you'll need to continually monitor analytics and make changes as necessary to optimize your sales and customer experience.

Cost and Benefit

When it comes to selling online courses of other creators, there are definitely some costs and benefits to consider. On the one hand, there's definitely a financial investment involved in setting up your platform and promoting your courses. You'll need to pay for things like website hosting, marketing tools, and other expenses. Plus, you'll need to put in the time and effort to research potential courses and find reputable creators.

However, there are also some big benefits to selling online courses. For one, it can be a great way to earn money. With the right courses and a solid marketing strategy, you can potentially generate a lot of sales and make a decent income. Additionally, by selling online courses of other creators, you'll be able to offer a wide variety of content to your customers, which can help you attract a larger audience and make more sales.

Another benefit is that you don't have to create the course yourself, you can focus on the selling and marketing part. Additionally, you can also earn a commission on the sales, which can be a great way to earn money with minimal effort.

Overall, while there are some costs involved in selling online courses of other creators, there are also many benefits that can make it a great investment. Just make sure to do your research and choose courses that will appeal to your target audience, and you'll be well on your way to making money selling online courses!

Skills Required

With a high level of curiosity and interest, you decide to have a chat with your friend who has been successfully earning regular income through selling online courses of other creators. You're eager to understand the nitty-gritty of this venture and what it takes to earn consistent income in the same. Your friend, who has been in this business for some time, agrees to share his knowledge and experience with you. As you sit down for a cup of coffee, you dive into the conversation, ready to learn and take notes.

- **You**: Hey, so I've been thinking about starting to sell online courses of other creators. How have you been able to make it work so well for you?
- **Friend**: Oh, it's been great! But it definitely takes some skills and knowledge to make it a success.
- **You**: Like what?
- **Friend**: Well, first and foremost, you need to have a good understanding of the different types of online courses that are available and what niches are currently in demand. That way, you can choose the right courses to sell and target the right audience.
- **You**: Okay, makes sense. What else?
- **Friend**: You also need to be comfortable with technology and have a good understanding of how to use different platforms and tools. For example, you need to know how to set up and manage an e-commerce store or course hosting platform.
- **You**: Got it. And what about marketing and promotion?

- **Friend**: Yeah, that's a big one. You need to know how to develop a marketing strategy and use different channels to reach your target audience. Social media, email marketing, and even offline advertising can be effective.
- **You**: Wow, it sounds like a lot of work.
- **Friend**: It can be, but it's also really rewarding. And once you get the hang of it, it's not as hard as it seems. Plus, you get to turn your passion into profit and help others in the process.
- **You**: That's true. Thanks for the advice. I think I'm ready to give it a shot.
- **Friend**: No problem! Just remember, don't give up if it gets tough. The money you'll earn will be worth it.
- **You**: And, of course, it's always a good idea to have a back-up plan in case things don't work out. Like, maybe I'll start a gardening course and call myself "The Business Guru"
- **Friend**: (laughs) Good luck with that!
- **You**: Alright, so it sounds like you've got a pretty good handle on the skills required to sell online courses of other creators. But before I start, is there anything else I need to know?
- **Friend**: Just one thing - don't forget to have fun! Selling online courses can be a lot of work, but it can also be incredibly rewarding. And who knows, maybe one day you'll be the one teaching others how to do it.
- **You**: Ha! I'll make sure to keep that in mind. Thanks for the advice, buddy.
- **Friend**: No problem. Just remember, if you ever need any help, I'm always here for you.
- **You**: You're the best. I'll make sure to send you a commission for every course I sell.
- **Friend**: Hey, as long as the commission is in beer, I'm good!"

In summary, the conversation between you and your friend highlights the various skills and knowledge required to sell online courses of other creators successfully. These include understanding the different types of online courses and in-demand niches, comfort with technology and platforms, and the ability to develop a marketing strategy and use various channels to reach your target audience. Your friend also mentions that while it can be a lot of work, it can also be very rewarding and emphasizes the importance of not giving up and having a back-up plan in case things don't work out. The conversation ends with a reminder to have fun and enjoy the process, and a friendly reminder that your friend is always available to help.

Call-to-Action

So, what are you waiting for? Don't let the fear of the unknown hold you back from taking the first step towards financial freedom. With the right skills, knowledge, and determination, you can make a consistent income by selling online courses of other creators. Take the time to research profitable niches and in-demand courses, find reputable course creators, and develop a marketing strategy that will help you reach your target audience. Remember, this is an ongoing process, but with a little bit of hard work and patience, you can turn your passion into profit and help others in the process. Don't let this opportunity pass you by. Start today and take control of your financial future!

ᐅᐅᐅ

FIVE
WRITE AN E-BOOK

Your friend has recently published a book. The title is "How to make money fast?". You meet him on a sunny day. Here is an excerpt.

- **You**: "Hey, congrats on publishing your e-book! So, what is it all about?"
- **Friend**: "Thanks! It's all about how to make money fast. I've been interested in personal finance for a while now and I wanted to share some of the tips and tricks I've learned along the way."
- **You**: "Oh cool, I could definitely use some advice on that. So, what exactly is an e-book?"
- **Friend**: "An e-book, short for electronic book, is a digital version of a traditional book. It's like a PDF or a Word document that you can read on your computer, tablet, or smartphone. They're becoming increasingly popular because they're convenient and easy to access."
- **You**: "I see. So, it's like a book, but in digital format. That makes sense. I've been hearing more and more about e-books lately, are they really that popular?"
- **Friend**: "Yeah, they're definitely gaining traction. People love the convenience of being able to access them from anywhere and on any device. Plus, e-books are often cheaper than physical books, so they're a great option for people who want to save some money. And with the rise of self-publishing platforms like Amazon Kindle Direct Publishing or Udemy, it's become easy for anyone to become an author and reach a global audience."
- **You**: "Wow, I had no idea. I might have to consider writing an e-book myself one day. But, for now, I'm going to buy your book and see what tips you have for making money fast."

- **Friend**: "I'd love that! And I'm sure you'll find some useful information in there. Writing an e-book is a great way to share your knowledge and experience with others and make some extra cash on the side."
- **You**: "I'll definitely keep that in mind. Thanks for the info. So, does this mean I'll be able to afford that fancy car I've always wanted now?"
- **Friend**: "Ha! Well, it might not be a Ferrari, but who knows, with the tips in my e-book you might be able to afford a fancy bicycle instead."

As our conversation above illustrates, writing an e-book is a great way to share your knowledge, expertise and experience with others. With the rise of self-publishing platforms and the increasing popularity of e-books, it's become easier than ever for anyone to become an author and reach a global audience. Not only is it a great way to share your wisdom, but it can also be a profitable venture.

Just like your friend in the conversation, who turned his passion for personal finance into an e-book, you too can turn your passion into a book and help others in the process. Whether you're an expert in gardening, cooking, photography or any other field, there's someone out there who wants to learn from you. Don't let fear or uncertainty hold you back from sharing your knowledge and experience with the world.

So, if you've been thinking about writing an e-book, now is the time to take the plunge. Who knows, you might even be able to afford that fancy car or bicycle you've always wanted!

Why Write an E-Book?

So, you're thinking about writing an e-book? That's great! Not only is it a great way to share your knowledge and experience with others, but it can also be a profitable venture.

For starters, e-books are becoming increasingly popular, especially in recent years with the rise of self-publishing platforms like Amazon Kindle Direct Publishing and Udemy. This means that there's a growing audience out there who are looking for new and interesting e-books to read. And if your e-book is well-written and provides valuable information, there's a good chance it will be well-received by that audience.

Another great reason for writing an e-book is that it allows you to share your passions and interests with others. If you're an expert in a particular field, like gardening or cooking, or you have a unique perspective on a topic, like personal finance or travel, an e-book is a great way to share that with the world.

Also, writing an e-book can be a great way to establish yourself as an authority in your field. It demonstrates that you have a deep understanding of your topic and that you're willing to share that knowledge with others.

Lastly, writing an e-book can be a great way to make some extra cash on the side. Many self-publishing platforms, like Amazon Kindle Direct Publishing, allow you to set a price for your e-book and earn royalties each time it's sold. So, not only are you sharing your knowledge and experience with others, but you're also getting paid for it.

So, whether you're looking to share your knowledge, establish yourself as an authority in your field, or make some extra cash, writing an e-book is a great way to do it. Don't wait any longer to start writing and share your wisdom with the world!

Step-by-Step Guide

Choosing a topic for your e-book is one of the most important steps in the process. It's important to choose a topic that you're passionate about and knowledgeable in, as this will make the writing process easier and ensure that the final product is of high quality.

- **Identifying your area of expertise**: If you have experience and knowledge in stock trading, this can be a great topic for your e-book. As a stock trader, you likely have insights and strategies that could be beneficial to others looking to start trading or improve their trading skills.
- **Researching potential topics**: Once you have identified stock trading as your area of expertise, you can start researching potential topics within that area. Some examples could include "10 profitable stock trading strategies" , "How to trade in bear market" , "Risk management in stock trading" etc.
- **Narrowing down the final topic**: After researching potential topics, it's time to narrow down your options and choose a specific angle to take. For example, you may choose to focus on day trading strategies or options trading strategies, depending on your own expertise and experience. You could also consider factors such as the level of competition in the market and how you can differentiate your e-book from others.

Another example could be if you want to focus on new traders, you may choose to focus on the basics of stock trading and common mistakes new traders make and how to avoid them. It's important to choose a topic that is not only interesting to you but also has the potential to be of interest to others, and one that you can add value to.

- **Outlining and Planning:** After you have chosen your topic, it's important to create a detailed outline of your e-book. This will help you stay organized and ensure that your content flows logically. A good outline will include an introduction, main sections, and a conclusion. For example, in the case of your e-book on "10 Profitable Stock Trading Strategies" your main sections could be introduction to stock trading, different types of trading strategies, case studies and conclusion.

  - **I. Introduction**

    - Brief overview of the topic of stock trading
    - Purpose of the e-book and what readers can expect to learn

  - **II. Section 1: Introduction to Stock Trading**

    - Definition and explanation of stock trading
    - Different types of stock trading (day trading, swing trading, long-term investing)
    - Importance of understanding market trends and conditions

  - **III. Section 2: Different Types of Trading Strategies**

    - Description and explanation of 10 different profitable trading strategies
    - Pros and cons of each strategy
    - Examples and case studies of successful implementation of the strategies

  - **IV. Section 3: Case Studies**

    - In-depth analysis of real-life examples of successful stock trading
    - Discussion of the strategies used and the results achieved

- ◦ **V. Conclusion**

  - Summary of key takeaways from the e-book
  - Additional resources for further learning and development in stock trading
  - A call to action for readers to start implementing the strategies and achieving success in stock trading

- ◦ **VI. References**

  - List of sources used in the e-book for research and information

This outline is only an example, you can use it as a starting point to create your own unique outline depending on your knowledge on stock trading and what you want to share with the readers. Once you have a solid outline, you can start to create the content and fill in the details for each section.

- **Creating a detailed outline:** Once you have a general outline, you can start to create a more detailed one. This will help you organize your thoughts and ideas and make sure that you cover all the important points. For example, you could include specific strategies and examples in each section of your e-book to make it more engaging and informative. Here is an example of outline of book on "10 Profitable Stock Trading Strategies".

  - ◦ **I. Introduction**

    - Brief overview of the topic of stock trading
    - Purpose of the e-book and what readers can expect to learn

  - ◦ **II. Section 1: Introduction to Stock Trading**

    - Definition and explanation of stock trading
    - Different types of stock trading (day trading, swing trading, long-term investing)
    - Importance of understanding market trends and conditions

- Understanding market conditions

  - How to read stock charts
  - Identifying key indicators and patterns
  - How to use technical analysis

- Understanding market trends

  - How to spot market trends
  - How to identify bullish and bearish markets
  - How to use fundamental analysis

- **III. Section 2: Different Types of Trading Strategies**

- Description and explanation of 10 different profitable trading strategies
- Pros and cons of each strategy
- Examples and case studies of successful implementation of the strategies

  - Momentum Trading

    - Definition and explanation of momentum trading
    - How to identify momentum stocks
    - Pros and cons of momentum trading
    - Case study of a successful momentum trade

  - Breakout Trading

    - Definition and explanation of breakout trading
    - How to identify breakout stocks
    - Pros and cons of breakout trading
    - Case study of a successful breakout trade

  - Scalping

    - Definition and explanation of scalping
    - How to identify scalping opportunities

- Pros and cons of scalping
- Case study of a successful scalping trade

- **IV. Section 3: Case Studies**

  - In-depth analysis of real-life examples of successful stock trading
  - Discussion of the strategies used and the results achieved

    - Case study 1 - Successful day trading

      - Analysis of the strategy used
      - Discussion of the results achieved
      - Lessons learned

    - Case study 2 - Successful swing trading

      - Analysis of the strategy used
      - Discussion of the results achieved
      - Lessons learned

- **V. Conclusion**

  - Summary of key takeaways from the e-book
  - Additional resources for further learning and development in stock trading
  - A call to action for readers to start implementing the strategies and achieving success in stock trading

- **VI. References**

  - List of sources used in the e-book for research and information

- **Setting a writing schedule**: Once you have a detailed outline, it's important to set a writing schedule. This will help you stay on track and ensure that you make steady progress. You could set a daily or weekly goal for yourself, depending on how much time you have available. It's important to be realistic and not to overload yourself.

A writing schedule is an important tool to help you stay on track and make consistent progress in writing your e-book. Below is a sample schedule that you can use as a starting point:

Week	Task
1	Research and gather information for Introduction
2	Write and draft content for Introduction
3	Review and edit Introduction
4	Research and gather information for Chapter 1
5	Write and draft content for Chapter 1
6	Review and edit Chapter 1
7	Research and gather information for Chapter 2
8	Write and draft content for Chapter 2
9	Review and edit Chapter 2
10	Research and gather information for Conclusion
11	Write and draft content for Conclusion
12	Review and edit Conclusion
13	Finalize and proofreading of e-book

Sample Schedule

This schedule is just an example and you can adjust it as per your own schedule and writing pace. You can also add additional weeks if you need more time to research, write and edit your e-book. It's also important to remember that a writing schedule is a work in progress and you may need to make adjustments as you go along. The key is to be flexible and adaptable, but also to stay focused and dedicated to your goal of writing your e-book.

By following these steps, you'll be able to create a well-structured and informative e-book that will be of value to your readers. Remember to stay organized, motivated and stay true to your schedule, it will make the process of writing an e-book much easier.

Writing and Editing

Writing effectively is crucial when it comes to creating an e-book. A well-written e-book is more likely to be read, shared and even purchased. Here are some tips for writing effectively:

- **Plan your content**: Before you start writing, create an outline of your e-book. This will help you stay organized and ensure that your content flows logically.
- **Write in a conversational tone**: Write as if you're having a conversation with your reader. This will make your e-book more engaging and relatable.
- **Use simple language**: Avoid using jargon or complex words. Keep your language simple and easy to understand.
- **Use examples and stories**: Use real-life examples and stories to illustrate your points. This will make your e-book more relatable and interesting.
- **Keep it short and sweet**: Avoid writing too much. Keep your e-book short and to the point.

Proofreading and editing are also essential when it comes to creating an e-book. Proofreading is the process of reading your e-book and checking for grammatical, punctuation and spelling errors. Editing, on the other hand, is the process of revising your e-book to improve its overall quality. Here are some reasons why proofreading and editing are important:

- **Improve readability**: Proofreading and editing can help improve the readability of your e-book. This will make it more enjoyable for your readers.
- **Enhance credibility**: A well-proofread and edited e-book will enhance your credibility as an author.
- **Avoid embarrassment**: Proofreading and editing can help avoid embarrassing mistakes that could damage your reputation.
- **Increase sales**: A well-written e-book is more likely to be read, shared and even purchased. This can increase your sales.

In short, writing effectively and proofreading and editing your e-book are crucial steps in the e-book creation process. They can help improve the quality of your e-book, enhance your credibility as an author, and increase your sales. So, take the time to plan your content, write in a conversational tone, use simple language, use examples and stories, keep it short and sweet and proofread and edit your e-book before publishing.

Design and Formatting

Choosing the right format for your e-book is important as it will determine how your readers will access and read your content. The most popular formats for e-books are PDF, ePub, and MOBI.

- **PDF** (Portable Document Format) is a widely accepted format that is compatible with most devices and reading software. It's good for e-books with a lot of graphics, tables, and images.
- **ePub** (Electronic Publication) is a format that is optimized for e-readers such as the Kindle and Nook. It's a good choice for text-heavy e-books.
- **MOBI** (Mobipocket) is a format that is optimized for Kindle devices. It's similar to ePub and is a good choice for text-heavy e-books.

Designing the cover and layout of your e-book is also an important aspect of the formatting process. The cover is the first thing that readers will see and it needs to be visually appealing and representative of the content inside. It is also important to keep in mind that the cover design should be consistent with the e-book format you have chosen.

When it comes to the layout, it is important to choose a clean, easy-to-read design that will make the e-book more engaging and accessible. Use of headings, subheadings, bullet points, and images can help break up the text and make it more visually appealing.

In conclusion, choosing the right format and designing a visually appealing cover and layout are important steps in the e-book creation process. They will determine how readers will access and read your content, and can have a big impact on the success of your e-book. It is important to choose a format that is compatible with most devices and reading software, and to design a cover and layout that will make your e-book more engaging and accessible.

Publishing and Marketing

When it comes to publishing and marketing your e-book, there are several options available for self-publishing. These include:

- **Amazon Kindle Direct Publishing (KDP)** - This is a platform that allows you to self-publish your e-book in Kindle format and make it available for purchase on Amazon. It's a popular choice among self-publishers as it has a wide reach and is easy to use.
- **Apple iBooks Author** - This is a platform that allows you to self-publish your e-book in ePub format and make it available for purchase on the iBooks store. It's a good choice if you're targeting readers who use Apple devices.

- **Smashwords** - This is a platform that allows you to self-publish your e-book in multiple formats (including ePub, MOBI, and PDF) and make it available for purchase on a variety of online retailers such as Barnes & Noble, Kobo, and iBooks.
- **Draft2Digital** - This is another platform that allows you to distribute your e-book to multiple retailers, including Amazon, iBooks, and Kobo.

Amazon Kindle Direct Publishing (KDP) is a self-publishing platform offered by Amazon that allows authors and publishers to publish and distribute their e-books in the Kindle store. KDP is available worldwide and it is a free service to use. It allows authors to upload their e-book in a variety of formats, such as PDF, MOBI, and EPUB. Once uploaded, the e-book can be made available for purchase in the Kindle store, where it can be read on Kindle devices, as well as Kindle apps for smartphones, tablets, and computers. Hers is a guide for publishing your e-book on Amazon.

- **Create an Amazon KDP account**: First and foremost, you'll need to create an account on Amazon Kindle Direct Publishing (KDP) in order to publish your e-book. This can be done by visiting the KDP website and following the prompts to create an account.
- **Prepare your manuscript**: Before you can publish your e-book, you'll need to prepare your manuscript. This includes formatting your book to meet Amazon's guidelines, such as using a specific font and font size, and ensuring that your book is free of errors.
- **Convert your manuscript to an e-book format**: Next, you'll need to convert your manuscript into an e-book format that is compatible with KDP. This can be done using software such as Calibre or Kindle Create.
- **Add your book details**: Once your e-book is ready, you'll need to add details about your book such as title, author name, description, and keywords to the KDP platform.
- **Upload your e-book**: After adding the details, you'll be prompted to upload your e-book file to KDP. You can either upload a Word document, MOBI file or an ePub file.
- **Set the price and distribution**: You can set the price of your e-book and choose where you want to distribute it. You can choose to distribute to Amazon.com, Amazon.in and other countries.
- **Preview and publish**: Preview your e-book and make sure that everything looks good. Once you are satisfied with the preview, click on

the publish button. Your e-book will be live on Amazon for readers to purchase and download within 24 to 48 hours.

- **Promote your e-book**: Once your e-book is live on Amazon, it's time to promote it. You can do this by sharing the link on social media, reaching out to book bloggers and reviewers, and even running paid advertising campaigns.

Note: The steps may vary slightly depending on your location and the platform you are using, but the overall process of publishing an e-book on Amazon Kindle Direct Publishing (KDP) is similar.

Once your e-book is published, it's important to have a strategy for promoting and marketing it. Some strategies that you can use include:

- Building an author website or blog and using it to promote your e-book.
- Leveraging social media to promote your e-book and interact with readers.
- Using email marketing to promote your e-book and build a list of readers.
- Hosting giveaways and contests to generate buzz around your e-book.
- Building relationships with other authors and influencers in your niche.
- Creating a book trailer or video to promote your e-book.
- Offering a free sample or excerpt of your e-book to generate interest.
- Utilizing paid advertising options such as Google AdWords or Facebook ads to reach a wider audience.

It's important to remember that publishing and marketing an e-book can take time and effort, but with a well-crafted strategy, you can increase your chances of success.

Cost and Benefit of Writing an E-Book

Writing an e-book can be a great way to share your knowledge and expertise with a wider audience, and even turn it into a source of income. But, like any endeavor, it does come with its own set of costs and benefits.

On the one hand, the cost of whriting an e-book can be relatively low. All you really need is a computer and an internet connection to get started. However, depending on the length and complexity of your e-book, you may need to invest in additional tools or software, such as a graphic design program to create a cover or a professional editor to proofread and edit your work. These costs can add up, but they're generally worth it in the long run if you want to produce a high-quality e-book.

On the other hand, the benefits of writing an e-book can be significant. For one, it's a great way to establish yourself as an expert in your field and build your personal brand. Additionally, if you choose to sell your e-book, you can earn a passive income from it for years to come. Plus, writing an e-book can open up new opportunities, such as speaking engagements, consulting work, or even a full-time career as an author.

Ultimately, the decision to write an e-book is a personal one, and it depends on your goals and the amount of time, money, and effort you're willing to invest. If you're passionate about a topic and have something valuable to share, writing an e-book can be a great way to reach a wider audience and even make some money on the side. But if you're not ready to put in the work and have a little bit of fun, then it's probably not for you.

Skillsets Required for Writing the E-Book

Fueled with excitement and motivation, you make the decision to embark on the journey of writing your own book, and seek the advice and guidance of your accomplished author friend, to gain a better understanding of the effort and dedication required to bring a book to fruition.

- **You**: Hey man, how's it going? I saw on your social media that you just published a book, congratulations!
- **Friend**: Thanks, I'm feeling pretty good about it. It was definitely a lot of work, but it was worth it.
- **You**: Yeah, I bet. So, what kind of skills did you have to have to get it done?
- **Friend**: Well, for starters, you need to have pretty good writing skills. You need to be able to clearly convey your ideas and make them interesting for the reader.
- **You**: Yeah, that makes sense. What about research? Did you have to do a lot of research for your book?
- **Friend**: Definitely. I spent a lot of time reading and gathering information for my book. It was important to have accurate information and to present it in a way that was easy to understand.
- **You**: Gotcha. So, what about editing and proofreading? How did you handle that?

- **Friend**: I had to be really meticulous with editing and proofreading. I went through my book multiple times to make sure there were no errors and that it was as polished as possible. It's important to have a good eye for detail and to be able to spot mistakes.
- **You**: Yeah, that makes sense. So, what about the publishing and marketing side of things? How did you handle that?
- **Friend**: I used Amazon Kindle Direct Publishing, it's a platform that makes it easy to self-publish your e-book. As for marketing, I used social media and reached out to book bloggers to help get the word out about my book. It's important to have a good online presence and to be able to promote your book effectively.
- **You**: Wow, that's really impressive. I might have to look into writing my own book.
- **Friend**: Go for it! Just be prepared to put in the work and have a good sense of humor, because it's not always going to be easy.
- **You**: (laughing) Yeah, I'll keep that in mind. Thanks for the advice!
- **Friend**: Hey, but don't worry, writing an e-book isn't all work and no play. Think of it as a fun challenge, and remember, the more you write, the more you can earn. Plus, who knows, maybe one day you'll have a best-seller on your hands and be the one buying me drinks at the book launch party.

Call-to-Action

In summary, writing an e-book can be a fantastic way to share your knowledge and expertise with a wider audience, while also having the potential to generate additional income. From honing your writing skills to gaining a sense of accomplishment and even turning your passion into a business, the benefits of writing an e-book are many. So, if you have an idea for a book and a desire to share it with the world, don't wait any longer. Take the first step today and start writing your own e-book. You never know where it may take you. Keep in mind, writing an e-book takes effort and dedication, but the rewards can be well worth it. The process of writing can be a personal growth experience, as you will be developing your writing skills, research, and organization skills. It's also a great way to establish yourself as an authority in your field, and open up new opportunities for you. So don't let fear of the unknown or self-doubt hold you back, trust in yourself and your abilities, and take that first step towards creating your very own e-book.

ᐇᐇᐇ

SIX

BLOGGING

People often need help making their online presence, but what if I told you that after reading this chapter you will be able to make your online presence worthwhile and earn an income?

In this chapter we will focus on how you can channel an income from writing about your experiences and interests and sharing your opinions. Blogging is a Lucrative online business that ANYONE can start today! Blogging has become a good career choice, especially after the covid 19 pandemic. Blogs saw a gain of over 50% in traffic, thereby increasing the revenue of 35% of bloggers.

Before we dive into the practicality of Blogging, let's understand the difference between a blog and a website. To a layperson, a blog and a website are the same, but in practicality, there is a difference between the two.

A website is a collection of interconnected, publicly accessible Web pages with a common domain name for a variety of objectives, websites can be built and maintained by an individual, a group, a company, or an organisation.

A blog is an online journal or an informational website run by individuals or a group of individuals. A blog is a shortened version of a "weblog." Writing blogs gives one a platform to share their stories, interests, and thoughts, educate, and make a worthwhile online presence. Some very famous bloggers in India are:

1. Kritika Khurana a.k.a @thatbohogirl
2. Komal Pandey
3. Anuradha Goyal
4. Niranjan Das

5. Mallika Basu
6. Amit Agarwal

In conclusion, Blogging can be a great way to express yourself and earn money from your passions. By following the steps outlined in this chapter, you can start your own blog and turn it into a profitable online business. Remember that success in blogging takes time and effort, but with dedication and hard work, you can achieve your goals. So, what are you waiting for? Start blogging today and let the world hear your voice!

Why Blogging?

Blogging has become incredibly popular over the years for several reasons. One of the biggest draws of Blogging is the ability for anyone to start a blog and share their thoughts, ideas, and experiences with a global audience. With the increase in use of social media and the ease of creating a website, starting a blog and reaching a broad audience has always been challenging. Additionally, Blogging has become an excellent way for people to establish themselves as experts in their field, build a personal brand, and even earn an income through advertising, sponsored posts, and affiliate marketing. Moreover, it is also a great way to connect with like-minded people who share similar interests, make friends, and build communities. All this has contributed to the growth of Blogging and its continued popularity.

Step-by-Step Guide to Start Blogging

Now that we have established a purpose and have understood the reason behind starting a blog, let's explore the various steps from ideation to publication of your blog.

Steps to Begin Blogging

1. **Choose a blogging platform** - Several blogging platforms are available to cater to different needs and industries. A quick search on google will give you a list of other platforms to choose from. Platforms offer a variety of templates; design options and allow you to analyze your blog's performance which will help to monetize your content. There are many blogging platforms available, both free and paid. Here are some popular options (WordPress, Blogger, Wix, Medium, Ghost, Squarespace, Tumblr, Weebly, Joomla, Drupal).

2. **Create a blog name and pick a blog host** - A good blog name is an essential part of your blog as it helps create the first impression. The blog name, also known as your domain name, will be your address on the web. For example, www.merinspeaks.com. So, what do you want to call your blog? It could be YourName.com. It could be YourBusinessName.com, or perhaps it's a creative brand name you thought up. If you have difficulty finalizing your blog name, you can make it using naming tools like wordoid and Bluehost. Your website can live online thanks to a blog host's web server space. This tool places your blog's files, information, and website code on a server, enabling anybody at any location in the world to visit your site. Your blog won't be accessible to the public without a blog host. While selecting a hosting platform, consider Uptime, Bandwidth, and Customer Support.

3. **Discover the ideal niche:** To have a successful blog, you must have a specific audience to target; it not only brings clarity but also helps to focus. There are three significant steps to choosing the ideal niche that

helps monetize and grow your blog.Narrow down your interests Discover your targeted audienceAssess its profitability

4. **Brainstorm and write your first blog:** Your blog is now technically ready. It's time to start considering the topics you'll begin with. Try to imagine your readers' perspectives while you think about topics. You can use the following Questions to help you through the brainstorming process: What difficulties does my intended audience encounter? What are topics popular within my targeted audience?What traits does my intended audience have?

5. **Promote your Blog** - You'll need to develop original strategies to draw people to your website if you want to attract readers. Let's highlight how to publicize your blog and help it grow into a reliable source for earning money. Posting on social media, creating a blog newsletter, connecting with an established network, advertising your blog by participating in discussion forums, investing in sponsored advertisements, and experimenting with various content formats are a few ways you can promote your blog.

6. **Monetize your blog** - Blogging is a marathon and not a sprint; it is not an instant road to success and requires hard work and time. To have a successful blogging space, there must be smooth interconnection, flow, and sync between the business model, target audience, content, and marketing. An absence of this will disrupt the process and cause hindrance to the goal of earning an income out of Blogging. After creating an audience and good traffic with quality and relevant blogs use of Advertising, and sponsored content can be highly effective ways to monetize your blog.

Once you have chosen your topic, the next step is to write your inaugural blog post. For instance, "How to Make the Perfect Cup of Coffee at Home" is an excellent example of a well-structured blog. Take note of the different sections that the blog is divided into.

"*Title: How to Make the Perfect Cup of Coffee at Home*

- *Introduction: Coffee is a staple for many people, whether it's to start the day off right or as a midday pick-me-up. However, making a perfect cup of coffee can be a challenge, especially when you're doing it at home. In this post, we'll go through some tips and tricks to help you make the perfect cup of coffee right in your own kitchen.*

- ***Body:***

  - ***Start with fresh beans*** *- The quality of your coffee beans will make a big difference in the taste of your coffee. Look for fresh, high-quality beans that are roasted within the last two weeks for the best flavor.*

  - ***Grind your beans correctly*** *- Different brewing methods require different grind sizes. For example, a French press requires a coarse grind while a drip coffee maker needs a medium grind. Be sure to adjust your grinder to the correct setting for your brewing method.*

  - ***Measure your coffee and water*** *- Use the right ratio of coffee to water to get the perfect flavor. A general rule of thumb is to use two tablespoons of coffee for every six ounces of water.*

  - ***Use the right temperature*** *- The water temperature for brewing coffee should be between 195 and 205 degrees Fahrenheit. Using water that is too hot or too cold can affect the flavor of your coffee.*

  - ***Brew for the right amount of time*** *- Different brewing methods require different brewing times. A French press, for example, should brew for about four minutes, while a drip coffee maker should take around five minutes. Be sure to follow the instructions for your specific brewing method.*

- ***Conclusion:*** *By following these tips, you can make the perfect cup of coffee right at home. Experiment with different brewing methods and find what works best for you. With a little practice, you'll be able to enjoy a delicious cup of coffee every morning without ever leaving your house.*

In conclusion, blogging is a great way to share your ideas, experiences, and passions with the world. By following the steps outlined in this sample blog post, you can create content that is engaging, informative, and valuable to your readers. Remember to choose a niche that you are passionate about, research your topics thoroughly, and always aim to provide value to your audience. With time and dedication, you can develop a successful blog that not only helps you connect with like-minded individuals but also generates income. Happy blogging!

By now, you must have a good understanding of how to start Blogging. But to make sure you're on the right track, here are a few tips to keep in mind as you begin your blogging journey:

1. **Be consistent**: Consistency is key in Blogging. It's essential to post regularly and stick to a schedule, so your readers know when to expect new content from you.
2. **Engage with your readers**: Building a community around your blog is essential. Respond to comments and engage with your readers to build a loyal following.
3. **Learn from other bloggers:** Read other blogs in your niche to stay up-to-date on the latest trends, and take inspiration from the best bloggers in your field.
4. **Be authentic:** Be true to yourself and voice out your opinion. Blogging is all about connecting with your readers, and being authentic is the best way to do that.
5. **Measure and analyze your progress:** Use tools like Google Analytics that will help you track your blog's performance and make adjustments to improve your readership and engagement.

Cost and Benefit

Blogging can come with its own set of costs and benefits. On the one hand, starting and maintaining a blog can require a certain amount of time and effort. You'll need to develop content ideas, research and write your posts, and promote your blog through social media or other channels. Additionally, if you want to monetize your blog, you'll need to invest in a domain name and hosting and any tools or services you may need to help you run your blog.

On the other hand, Blogging can also be incredibly rewarding. Not only can it be an excellent way to part your thoughts, ideas, and experiences with the world, but it can also be a great way to build your brand and establish yourself as an authority in your niche. Additionally, if you're able to grow a sizable audience, you can also monetize your blog through advertising, sponsored posts, or affiliate marketing.

Overall, Blogging can be a great way to build your brand, share your ideas and experiences with the world, and even make money. But like any other venture, it takes effort and dedication to be successful.

Skills Required

Developing the skills necessary to become a blogger is crucial, and equivalent to solid writing abilities. The skills listed below are vital for producing valuable and exciting content that will draw readers and keep them coming back for more.

1. **Research:** You must thoroughly understand your subject matter and keep up-to-date with current events to provide informative and engaging material.
2. **SEO:** To increase traffic to your blog, search engine optimization (SEO) is essential. Your blog will rank higher in search results and draw more readers if you know how to optimize your blog.
3. **Marketing:** Writing a blog involves both developing and promoting content. It's critical to comprehend the many marketing platforms you might use to advertise your blog and draw users.
4. **Social media:** Understanding how to use social media sites like Facebook, Twitter, Instagram, and Pinterest to promote your blog and interact with readers
5. **Graphic design and photography:** Basic graphic design and photography skills can help you create visually appealing content that will make your blog stand out.
6. **Networking:** Because Blogging is a community, establishing relationships with other bloggers in your specialized field can increase your viewership and expose you to new business opportunities.

Call-to-Action

We can agree that writing Blogs is a good side income choice; take your love of writing into a successful side business. Create a blog now and discover how to monetize it to generate passive income regularly. Blogging is a fantastic way to share your stories, interests, and thoughts and educate and make a worthwhile online presence. It also helps you create your unique brand a blog is a fantastic venue for showcasing your abilities and knowledge, helping you stand out from the competition and leaving a positive impression on potential employers. You can also earn money from your readers with consistency and intelligent work. Owners of blogs also have the option to sell their goods and services, run advertisements, or write sponsored blog entries. So what are you waiting for? Join the bloggers club to open a new effective stream of income.

ᗺᗺᗺ

SEVEN
CAR RENTALS

Earn anytime, anywhere by just driving! Sounds great.

By partnering with a car rental company as a driver, you can earn as much as you desire. The more you drive, the more money you can make. This is an excellent opportunity for those who want to earn extra income or even make a full-time career out of it. With flexible hours and the ability to set your schedule, it's a perfect way to earn money on your terms. So, if you're looking for a way to earn extra cash, consider becoming a rental car driver. The earning potential is unlimited.

In this chapter, we're diving into the world of driving for cash, baby! Specifically, we'll discuss how partnering with a car rental company can help you earn some serious dough. You might be thinking, "Why would anyone willingly choose to be a driver when there are so many other options out there?" Well, my friend, you're about to find out. Buckle up because we're about to take a wild ride through the benefits of being a rental car driver. And don't worry; there will be plenty of jokes and puns along the way. So, let's get behind the wheel and rev up our engines because this will be a gas! (Yes, I went there).

Why Partner With a Car Rental Company?

India is a developing nation, and people's standard of living is increasing. People in India are more inclined towards luxury, but affordability comes into the picture. Not every common person can afford a car; even if he can, the maintenance and sales cost becomes a huge concern.

According to reports, the car rental industry has shown significant growth. People use these services daily, allowing them to enjoy luxury and reach their destination at pocket-friendly prices. There is a massive demand for this service in metro cities. The major players in this industry are Ola, Uber, and Meru cabs.

Becoming a driver partner with a car rental company has many benefits. You earn a good income from this source and enjoy other benefits like being your boss concerning the flexibility to choose the location and working timings. The driver also has the flexibility to do a part-time job, and they can log out according to their driving capacity.

From the driver's perspective, a ride yields around 200 rupees, and completing 20 such rides in a day can help him earn 4000 per day, which is 1,20,000 per month. After deducting the fee charged by the provider and fuel, the margin is 40%, equal to roughly 50,000 per month. This is a decent income.

Step-by-Step Guide to Becoming a Driving Partner with a Car Rental Company

You can quickly sign up with a car rental company with minimal requirements. The process for the same has been elaborated below:

1. **Researching potential car rental companies**: The first step in becoming a driving partner with a car rental company is to study available options. In India, some popular car rental companies include Ola, Uber, Rapido, etc. Look at the company's reputation, their requirements, and the type of cars they offer. For example, Ola offers vehicles for both personal and commercial use, while Rapido specializes in bike rentals.
2. **Meeting the eligibility criteria**: Each car rental company has its own eligibility criteria that a driver-partner must meet before becoming a driving partner. This can include having a valid driver's license, having a specific type of car, and passing a background check. For example, to become a driving partner with Ola, you must have a valid driver's license and a four-wheeler vehicle and pass a background verification process.
3. **Signing up and undergoing training**: Once you've determined that you meet the eligibility criteria, the next step is to sign up to become a driving partner. This can typically be done online and may involve completing an application and undergoing training. For example, Ola provides an online application process, and once you're selected, you need to undergo a training session that includes both online and offline training.

4. **Starting to drive**: Once you've completed the necessary paperwork and training, you'll be ready to drive and earn money as a driving partner. For example, once you complete the training, the driver partner provides you with a car rental kit, including a mobile phone and a SIM card, and you'll be able to start accepting customer rides.

5. **Monitoring earnings and optimizing your driving**: As a driving partner, it's essential to regularly monitor your earnings and make adjustments as needed to optimize your driving. This can include driving during peak hours, accepting longer rides, or focusing on specific areas. For example, if you're earning more money by driving during peak hours, you can plan your driving schedule accordingly.

6. **Customer service:** Good customer service is essential for a successful driving partnership. This can include being punctual, maintaining the cleanliness of your car, and being friendly and helpful to your customers. For example, if you receive positive customer feedback, you may be eligible for a higher rating, resulting in more ride requests and higher earnings.

Following these steps, you can become a driving partner with Ola or any other company and earn money by providing rides to customers. Remember to meet the eligibility criteria, complete the onboarding process, attend the training session, provide good customer service, maintain your vehicle, and keep track of your earnings.

Payment Model of Ola

The payment model for Ola partners (drivers) is based on a combination of factors, including distance travelled, time spent on the trip, and the vehicle used.

Here's a breakdown of the different types of fares and their corresponding rates:

Fare Type	Distance (km)	Time (min)	Base Fare	Per KM Fare	Per Min Fare
Micro	Up to 5	Up to 20	₹40	₹6	₹1
Mini	Up to 10	Up to 30	₹60	₹9	₹1.5
Sedan	Up to 15	Up to 40	₹80	₹12	₹2
Prime	Up to 20	Up to 50	₹100	₹15	₹2.5

Breakdown of Ola Fare

In addition to the base fare and distance/time charges, Ola partners also earn a commission on each trip. This commission varies depending on the type of vehicle and the city, but it is typically around 20%.

For example, if a partner completes a Micro trip of 5 km in 20 minutes, the driver-partner would calculate the fare as follows:

- Base Fare: Rs. 40
- Distance Fare: (5 km x Rs. 6/km) = Rs. 30
- Time Fare: (20 min x Rs. 1/min) = Rs. 20
- Commission: (Rs. 90 x 20%) = Rs. 18
- Total Earnings: Rs. 90 + Rs. 18 = Rs. 108

It is to be noted that the above fare table is just an example and the fare may vary based on the city and on the time of the day.

The potential of earning as an Ola driver in India can vary depending on several factors, including the city you're driving in, the time of day, and your driving experience. However, Ola drivers in India can earn anywhere from INR 20,000 to INR 50,000 per month.

It's important to note that Ola drivers are independent contractors, which means they are responsible for their expenses, such as fuel, maintenance, and taxes. Additionally, the income can vary depending on how much time and effort you put into driving. The more you drive, the more you can earn.

Ola drivers can take advantage of peak hours, surge pricing, and bonuses to maximize their earning potential. For example, during peak hours such as rush hour or weekends, there is usually a higher demand for rides and, therefore, higher fares. Surge pricing also applies during these times, which can increase fares even further. Additionally, Ola offers bonuses for completing a certain number of rides in a given period, which can boost earnings.

Overall, the earning potential as an Ola driver in India can be pretty substantial, but it requires effort and dedication. By understanding the market and taking advantage of peak hours, surge pricing, and bonuses, Ola drivers can maximize their earning potential.

Costs to be Incurred

When it comes to becoming a driving partner with a car rental company like Ola, there are certain costs that the driver will need to keep in mind. These costs include:

- **Vehicle cost**: The driver will need to have a vehicle that meets the requirements set by Ola. This can include expenses such as purchasing or leasing a new car and ongoing maintenance and repairs costs.
- **Insurance**: The driver will be responsible for obtaining insurance for the vehicle, which can include liability insurance and commercial insurance if required.
- **Fuel costs**: The driver will need to cover the fuel for their vehicle while on the job.
- **Vehicle maintenance**: The driver will need to cover the cost of regular maintenance and repairs for their vehicle, such as oil changes, tire rotations, and brakes.
- **Ola commission**: The driver has to pay a commission to Ola on every ride they give to Ola's customer. This commission varies depending on the city and the type of vehicle.

It's essential to keep in mind that these costs can vary depending on the location, type of vehicle, and how much you drive. However, with the potential to earn a good income as an Ola driver in India, many people find the costs worth it in the long run.

Benefits

There are several benefits involved for a driver when partnering with a car rental company such as Ola in India. Some of these include:

- **Flexible working hours**: Drivers can choose when and how often they work, allowing for a balance between earning an income and other commitments.
- **Increased earning potential**: With a larger pool of customers, drivers can make more than they would with traditional taxi or ride-sharing services.
- **Insurance coverage**: Ola provides insurance coverage for drivers and their vehicles, providing peace of mind and protection in case of accidents or other incidents.
- **Access to training and support**: Ola offers a range of training and support options for drivers, including onboarding and safety training and 24/7 customer support.
- **Tax benefits**: As self-employed contractors, drivers may be eligible for certain tax deductions based on their expenses related to driving.
- **Cost savings**: Partnering with a car rental company like Ola can help drivers save money on maintenance, fuel, and other expenses.
- **Brand recognition**: Ola is a well-known and reputable brand in India, which can help drivers attract more customers and build their reputation as professional drivers.

Overall, partnering with a car rental company like Ola can be an excellent way for drivers to earn a steady income while enjoying the flexibility and freedom of being self-employed.

Skills Required

Skills required for becoming an Ola driver in India include:

- Good driving skills and knowledge of local roads and traffic laws.
- Strong customer service skills to interact with passengers and address any issues.
- Good communication skills, as the driver will need to communicate with the Ola support team and passengers.
- Knowledge of how to use the Ola app and GPS navigation systems.
- Time management skills to ensure that pickups and drop-offs are made on time.
- Flexibility and adaptability: The driver may need to adjust their schedule to meet the ride demand.

- Basic vehicle maintenance skills to ensure the car is in good working condition and safe for passengers.
- Strong problem-solving skills to deal with unexpected situations on the road.
- Knowledge of local languages to communicate effectively with passengers.
- Good understanding of the industry trends, rules, and regulations related to car rentals and ride-hailing services

It's worth noting that as Ola continues to grow and evolve, the above list of skills may change, and it's essential to stay updated with the company's policies and requirements.

Call-to-Action

If you're interested in becoming a driving partner with a car rental company like Ola, now is the perfect time to take action. With the right skills and a willingness to put in the work, you can turn your passion for driving into a profitable career. Whether you're looking to supplement your current income or make a full-time career out of it, partnering with a car rental company like Ola can be a great option. So, don't wait any longer. Take the first step and apply to become a driving partner today!

ϷϷϷ

EIGHT
DATA ENTRY

Data entry is a pretty cool gig. Not only does it offer flexible hours, but it also pays based on your productivity. Plus, it's a great way to earn extra cash if you already have a day job.

And let's remember; you get paid to type! How awesome is that? You can work on your typing skills and earn money at the same time.

So, if you're looking for a way to make some extra dough and have some spare time, data entry might be the perfect gig for you. Ensure you've decent typing skills and are good to go. Give it a shot; what do you have to lose?

There can be two possible situations that you may be in.

Case 1: If you are a fresher and need to gain knowledge or experience in the field but want to start working as a data entry expert. The following are the requirements you must possess:

1. Learn how to use basic office tools such as computers, scanners, copiers, printers, and calculators;
2. Gain proficiency with database software, spreadsheets, and word processing;
3. Have a firm grasp of language and punctuation;
4. Learn how to enter numbers accurately.
5. Work on your data entry and keyboarding abilities.

Case 2: If you are starting and wish to advance in the field of data entry with basic knowledge, Then these tips will be helpful to you:

1. Work on your fundamental data entry abilities.

2. Must be able to enter data quickly and accurately and try innovative data input techniques to quicken the process and minimize mistakes.
3. Consistently practice typing between 50 and 80 words per minute.

Data entry is an incredibly far-reaching field. Data entry jobs are known by a variety of names, such as data entry specialists, data entry clerks, or information processing workers.

Why Data Entry as a Source of Income

Data entry can be a great source of income because it offers flexibility. You can work from anywhere and at any time if you have a computer and a stable internet connection. Plus, the pay is often based on the work you complete, so the more you work, the more you can earn. It's also an excellent option for people looking for a side hustle or a way to make extra money. And let's remember, and it's a great way to turn your typing skills into cash. With data entry, you can work at your own pace and make money while doing something you're good at. Plus, it doesn't require a degree or specific qualifications, making it an excellent option for people from all backgrounds. Overall, data entry is a great way to make money while having flexibility in your schedule and the freedom to work from anywhere.

Step-by-Step Guide

Once you have acquainted yourself with the requirements or tips from the situations mentioned above, whichever fits your boat, it's time to dive deeper into the steps on how to become a Data Entry Professional.

1. **Research**: The first step to making money through data entry is researching the various available opportunities. Look for companies or websites that offer data entry jobs in India, such as Freelancer, Upwork, or Indeed.
2. **Register and create a profile**: Once you've identified potential opportunities, register with the company or website and create a profile. Include your typing speed, relevant skills and experience, and any certifications you may have.
3. **Apply for jobs**: Once your profile is set up, apply for jobs matching your skills and experience. Make sure you tailor your cover letter and resume

to the specific job you aim to apply.

4. **Complete tests and interviews**: Some companies may require you to complete a typing test or interview as part of the application process. Be prepared to demonstrate your skills and experience.

5. **Start working**: Once you've been selected for a job, start working on the data entry tasks assigned to you. Make sure to adhere to the guidelines and deadlines provided.

6. **Get paid**: Upon completing the tasks, you will be paid for your work. The payment method may vary depending on the company or website you are working for.

By following this step-by-step guide, you can start earning money through data entry in India while working from the comfort of your home. With research and effort, you can find the right opportunity and earn a steady income through data entry.

Examples

A data entry professional can work for a company like Quikr, which is an Indian classifieds platform that offers data entry jobs for entering classified ads into the website.

Another opportunity is to work for a company like 2Captcha, a captcha-solving service that hires data entry professionals to solve captchas as part of their service.

A person can earn by working as a data entry operator for a company like Amazon, which hires data entry professionals to update and maintain product information on their website.

The Payment Model

The payment model for data entry jobs can vary depending on the employer and the type of work being done. Some standard payment models include:

1. **Hourly rate**: This is the most common payment model for data entry jobs. The employee is paid a set hourly rate for the time they spend working on data entry tasks.

2. **Piece rate**: In this model, the employee is paid a certain amount for each data they enter. This can be based on the number of words typed, the

number of forms filled out, or the number of data points entered.

3. **Project-based**: In this model, the employee is paid a fixed amount for completing a specific project or set of data entry tasks. This is often used for large projects that require a significant amount of data entry work.
4. **Commission-based**: Some data entry jobs pay a commission based on the number of sales or leads generated from the data entered.

It's important to note that, in India, data entry jobs are often paid on a project basis, and the rate for the project is fixed. Some companies also pay hourly, but the pay is generally low.

Work Involved

Data entry transcribes information into another medium, usually through input into a computer program. It is used in various industries, including banking and IT companies, and can be a flexible and profitable source of income for those who possess the necessary skills.

1. Typing and transcribing information from various sources, such as handwritten documents, spreadsheets, and numerical sequences
2. Entering data into computer programs such as Microsoft Excel or database systems
3. Verifying and checking data for accuracy and completeness
4. Updating and maintaining existing data
5. Following specific guidelines and instructions for formatting and inputting data
6. Communicating with clients or team members to clarify information or resolve any issues
7. Keeping track of work progress and meeting deadlines for projects.

Data entry can be a great way to earn extra income while working from home. It is a flexible and goal-based job allowing you to work at your pace and schedule. However, it is essential to be proficient in typing, follow instructions, and have attention to detail to succeed in this field. Data entry is worth considering if you are looking for a way to earn money from home.

Cost

The cost involved in a data entry job mainly includes equipment such as a computer or laptop, an internet connection, and any software or programs required. In some cases, there may be costs incurred for training or certification. Additionally, there may be costs for setting up a home office or creating a suitable workspace if working from home. However, many companies may provide equipment and training, so it is essential to check with the employer before starting the job.

Benefits

In today's time and period, Data Entry is very significant and has several advantages; the well-known benefits are listed below:

- Many sectors, including IT, healthcare, administrative, accounting and finance, government, retail, and sales, need data entry specialists.
- The remuneration is appealing and is based on various parameters, including talents, experience, job responsibilities, etc.
- You can also work as a part-time data entry clerk after completing senior secondary
- It serves as a fantastic source of additional money.
- Data Entry is a very flexible job to do, as you can work as a freelancer
- Data entry jobs provide multiple benefits, including working from a suitable location, setting your schedule, and other

Skills Required

Data entry is majorly concerned with converting primary data into data that a company can use. Proper formatting, rearranging, and adding essential elements to the data can make it more useful. The data entry job is relatively easy, but the task becomes repetitive. Becoming a data entry professional requires a few soft skills, which you must learn.

- Strong typing skills and proficiency in keyboard shortcuts
- Good attention to detail and accuracy in data entry
- Basic knowledge of computer programs and software, such as Microsoft Office Suite (Word, Excel, etc.)
- Familiarity with databases and data management systems

- Strong organizational skills and the ability to multitask
- Proficient writing and verbal communicating skills to communicate with clients and colleagues
- Ability to work independently and meet deadlines in a fast-paced environment
- Basic understanding of data privacy and security protocols
- Prior experience in similar roles or related fields is a plus.

Call-to-Action

So, Are you ready to take the first step toward earning money through data entry? With the right skills and a little hard work, you can start earning a steady income in no time. Whether you're looking to add on to your current income or create a new career, data entry is a great option. With the flexibility to not only work from home but also set your schedule, you can easily fit data entry work into your busy lifestyle. So, why wait? Start looking for data entry opportunities today, and take control of your financial future. Don't let the fear of not having the right skills stop you from pursuing this opportunity. With online training and tutorials readily available, you can easily acquire the skills required for the job. Don't hesitate; take action today and earn money through data entry!

❦❦❦

NINE

SELLING HOMEMADE/ HANDMADE ITEMS

Have you ever thought about turning your hobby into a business? Have you ever looked at your homemade crafts or food products and thought, "I could sell this"? Well, now is the time to make that thought a reality! With the rise of online marketplaces and social media, it's easier than ever to start your own home-based business.

From homemade candles and crocheted items to home baking and wax seal stamping, the possibilities are endless. Not only is it a great way to earn some extra income, but it also allows you to share your passion and creativity with the world. The handmade and homemade business is a popular concept because it offers uniqueness, high quality, and the ability to customize products. Plus, you can rest easy knowing that your products are sustainable and eco-friendly.

So, why not give it a shot? With a little investment, you could be on your way to turning your hobby into a successful business. Don't let fear hold you back. The internet has made it possible for anyone to start a business from the comfort of their own home. The earning potential is huge! So, take the first step today and start turning your hobby into a business.

Are you tired of just having a hobby that doesn't seem to bring in any money? Well, it's time to change that! In this chapter, we'll dive into the exciting world of turning your passion into profit. From crafting to cooking, the possibilities are endless when it comes to turning your hobby into a money-making venture. So, buckle up and get ready to learn how to take that hobby of yours and turn it into a successful business right from the comfort of your own home.

Why Start a Homemade/Handmade Business?

Are you tired of working a 9-5 job and looking for a way to turn your passion into profit? Have you ever thought about starting your own homemade or handmade business? With the rise of e-commerce platforms like Etsy and Amazon Handmade, it's never been easier to turn your hobby into a successful business.

Not only is starting a homemade or handmade business a great way to earn extra income, but it also allows you to be creative and express yourself in a way that traditional jobs may not. Plus, you get to be your own boss and work from the comfort of your own home.

But that's not all. By starting a homemade or handmade business, you're also supporting the local and global economy by promoting sustainable and ethical practices. And with the increased demand for unique and high-quality products, there's never been a better time to turn your hobby into a business.

So why not give it a try? You never know, your homemade candles or crocheted blankets could be the next big thing.

Step-by-Step Guide to Starting a Homemade/Handmade Business

Let's check out the 10 steps that will help anyone who is ready to convert their hobby of craft and culinary into a business

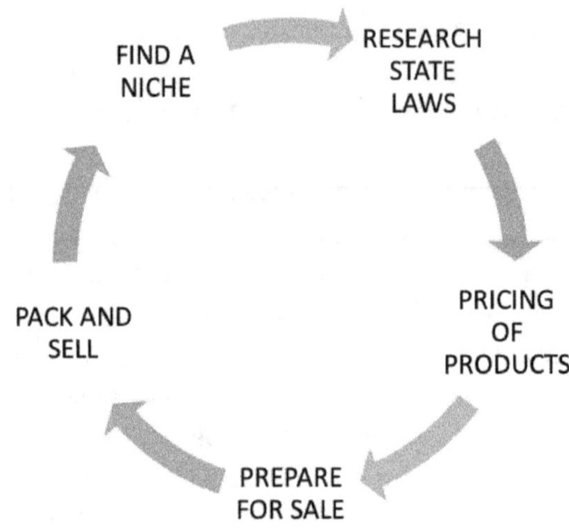

Steps to Convert Hobby of Craft and Culinary into Business

1. **Start by creating a list** of all the things you are skilled at making. This can be anything from baking cakes to making candles, crocheting blankets, or creating wax seal stamps.
2. **Research the market trends** for the products on your list. This will give you an idea of the demand for each item and help you narrow down your options.
3. **Make an investment** in your business. This can include buying equipment, materials, or hiring staff if necessary.
4. **Research the competition** in these markets. Look at what other businesses are offering similar products and try to find ways to differentiate yourself.
5. **Determine how much you want to make:** Set realistic financial goals for your business and create a plan to achieve them.
6. **Decide on your target audience**: Identify the people who are most likely to be interested in your products and create a marketing strategy to reach them.
7. **Create an online presence**: This can include a website, social media accounts, or an online marketplace.

8. **Start selling your products**: This can be done through online marketplaces, social media, or by setting up a store or booth at a local market or craft fair.
9. **Continuously improve your product and service**: Keep up with the competition and trends and improve your product and service to meet the customer demand.
10. Finally, **don't forget to have fun** and enjoy the process of turning your hobby into a business!

Cost

Starting a homemade/handmade business can vary in cost depending on the type of product or service you offer. Here are a few examples of potential costs to consider:

- **Materials**: Depending on what you're making, you'll need to invest in materials such as fabric, yarn, paint, wax, etc.
- **Tools**: Depending on what you're making, you'll need certain tools like a sewing machine, knitting needles, wax melting pot, etc.
- **Packaging and shipping**: If you plan on selling your products online, you'll need to invest in packaging materials like boxes, bubble wrap, and shipping labels.
- **Website and marketing**: To reach more customers, you may need to invest in creating a website and paying for marketing efforts like social media ads, flyers, or email campaigns.
- **Legal and insurance**: Depending on your business and the type of products you're selling, you may need to invest in legal fees for registering your business and getting insurance.

Keep in mind that these are just a few examples of potential costs, and your business may require additional expenses. It's important to research the costs associated with the specific type of business you're starting and create a budget accordingly.

Benefits

Starting a homemade or handmade business has several benefits. One of the main benefits is that it allows you to turn your passion into a source of income. You get to make money while doing something you enjoy. Additionally, there is a high demand for unique, handmade products, and you can set your own prices, which can be higher than mass-produced goods.

Another benefit is that you have full control over your business. You decide when and how much to work, giving you a good work-life balance. It also allows you to work from home, saving on expenses such as rent and transportation.

Starting a homemade or handmade business also allows you to be creative and innovative. You can experiment with different designs and products, and you can personalize your products to make them unique. Furthermore, it is an eco-friendly and sustainable way of doing business.

Lastly, it is a low-cost business to start. You do not need a lot of money to get started. With minimal startup costs and low overhead, you can begin to make a profit relatively quickly. It is a great way to test the waters of entrepreneurship without a large investment.

Call-to-Action

Selling your work online is a great way of not only showcasing your talent but also earning a side income, it only just demands hard work, consistency, planning, dedication and desire it makes big things happen. To start selling homemade/handmade items it is necessary to not only commercial and marketing aspects of the product but also the technical aspects of setting up a website or online store, capturing and editing attractive photographs, creating strong SEO, and sending email newsletters. You must develop your selling skills and manage to meet the wants and issues of your clients. You must understand your brand's narrative and know how to convey it. You must develop your social media marketing skill.

ppp

TEN

FREELANCING

Are you tired of the 9-5 grind and looking for a way to make money on your own terms?

Freelancing might just be the perfect solution for you! As a freelancer, you have the flexibility to work when and where you want, and to choose the projects that align with your skills and interests. It's a great way to gain experience, build your portfolio, and earn a good income. In this guide, we'll walk you through the steps of starting your own freelancing business, from finding your niche to landing your first clients. Whether you're a writer, designer, programmer, or any other type of creative professional, freelancing can be a great way to take control of your career and your income.

So, let's dive in and get started on your freelancing journey!

How Does Freelancing Work?

Managing contractual work for several clients or businesses is part of freelancing. Freelancers are self-employed people who aren't always fully dedicated to a single company.

In this field, clients pay by the hour, by the work, or by the project, based on the conditions that were previously agreed upon. Freelancers can work in a wide range of industries, including teaching, social media, programming, marketing, and content development.

India is ranked as one of the fastest-growing freelancing markets globally and has 15 million freelance workers.

Step-by-Step Guide on How to Start Freelancing

Are you tired of working a 9-5 job and want to take control of your own schedule and income? Freelancing may be the solution for you. But where do you even start? Here's a step-by-step guide on how to turn your skills into a successful freelancing career:

- **Begin with listing down 10 to 15 of your interests and passions**. If you work in a field you are passionate about, you are less likely to leave it when times are rough. Some examples are listed below:

  - Writing (content creation, copywriting, technical writing, etc.)
  - Graphic design
  - Web development
  - Digital marketing
  - Photography
  - Translation
  - Consulting
  - Video production
  - Audio production
  - Virtual assistance
  - Data entry
  - Social media management
  - Event planning
  - Tutoring
  - Coaching
  - and many more.

- **Determine your skills and expertise**: Before starting your freelancing journey, it's important to identify the specific skills and services you can offer to potential clients. For example, if you're a photographer, your skills could include portrait photography, event photography, and editing.
- **Build your portfolio**: A portfolio is a great way to showcase your work and attract potential clients. Make sure to include high-quality images or videos of your work and add detailed captions to provide context.
- **Create a website or online presence**: Having a website or online profile is essential for freelancers. It's a great way to establish your brand and

make it easy for clients to find and contact you.

- **Network and market yourself**: Networking and marketing are crucial for freelancers. Reach out to potential clients, attend industry events, and use social media to promote your services.
- **Set your rates**: Decide on a pricing structure that works for you and your clients. Be sure to consider your experience, the cost of living in your area, and the rates of other freelancers in your field.
- **Find clients**: Finding clients can be one of the most challenging parts of freelancing. Reach out to friends, family, and past colleagues for referrals. Also, you can use online platforms like Upwork and Freelancer, to find clients. Here is an example of finding clients on **Upwork**.

  - First, **create a profile on Upwork** that showcases your photography skills and experience. Make sure to include a portfolio of your past work and any relevant certifications or education.
  - Next, **search for photography job opportunities** on Upwork by using relevant keywords in the search bar.
  - Once you find a job that interests you, make sure to **read the job posting carefully** to ensure that you meet the requirements and qualifications.
  - Before you submit a proposal, make sure to **tailor your proposal to the specific job and client**. Be sure to highlight your relevant experience and skills, and explain how you can add value to the project.
  - Once you submit your proposal, you may need to **wait for the client to review and accep**t it. Be patient and be prepared to follow-up with the client if necessary.
  - Once the client accepts your proposal, you can **start working on the project** and communicating with the client through Upwork's messaging system.
  - Keep in mind that **building a good reputation** on Upwork takes time, so be sure to deliver **high-quality work** and always communicate professionally and promptly with clients. This will help you gain positive reviews, which will increase your chances of getting hired for future projects.

- **Manage your finances**: Freelancing requires you to keep track of your income and expenses. Be sure to set aside money for taxes and keep detailed records of all your financial transactions.

- **Continuously improve your skills**: As a freelancer, it's important to continuously improve your skills and stay up-to-date with the latest industry trends. Take online courses, attend workshops, and seek feedback from clients to improve your work.

Benefits of Freelancing

Freelancing can offer several benefits, including:

1. **Flexibility**: Freelancers can often set their own schedule and work from anywhere, allowing them to balance work and personal responsibilities more easily.
2. **Control over workload**: Freelancers can choose which projects they want to work on, and can often negotiate their own rates and deadlines.
3. **Variety of work**: Freelancers can often work on a variety of projects, which can help them develop new skills and expand their portfolio.
4. **Tax benefits**: Freelancers can often deduct business-related expenses from their taxes, which can help lower their overall tax bill.
5. **Opportunities for growth**: Freelancing can provide opportunities for entrepreneurs, who can then grow their own businesses.
6. **Networking**: Freelancing can help you to build a strong professional network, which can lead to new job opportunities.
7. **Autonomy**: Freelancing gives you the freedom to make your own decisions, and can be a great way to work independently and be in charge of your own career.

Costs Incurred

There are several costs that may be incurred when starting a freelancing business, including:

1. **Equipment**: You may need to purchase equipment such as a computer, printer, internet connection, and other office supplies.
2. **Software**: Depending on your field, you may need to purchase software programs or subscriptions in order to complete your work.

3. **Office space**: Some freelancers may choose to rent an office space, although it's not required.
4. **Legal and accounting fees**: You may need to pay for legal services or an accountant to set up and maintain your business.
5. **Marketing and advertising**: You may need to invest in marketing and advertising to promote your business and attract new clients.

It's worth noting that some of these costs can be minimized by working from home and also some of the costs may not be applicable to your field. It's always good to research and plan your expenses before starting freelancing.

Skills Required to Freelance

There are a variety of skills that can be beneficial for freelancers, depending on the field they are working in, but some of the most important skills include:

1. **Expertise in a specific field**: Freelancers typically need to have a high level of skill and knowledge in the field they are working in, whether it be writing, programming, graphic design, etc.
2. **Time management**: Freelancers are responsible for managing their own time and workload, so good time management skills are essential.
3. **Communication**: Freelancers need to be able to effectively communicate with clients and other professionals in order to negotiate rates and deadlines, and to provide updates on the progress of their work.
4. **Adaptability**: Freelancers often work on a variety of projects, so being able to adapt to different work environments, client needs, and project requirements is important.
5. **Self-Motivation**: Freelancers need to be able to motivate themselves to work and meet deadlines, as they may not have the structure and support of a traditional workplace.
6. **Business acumen**: Freelancers are running their own businesses, so having knowledge of business management, accounting, and marketing is essential.
7. **Technical skills**: Depending on the field, freelancers may need to have knowledge of specific software, programming languages, or other technical skills in order to complete their work.

8. **Networking**: Freelancers need to be able to build and maintain a professional network in order to find new clients and job opportunities.

Call-to-Action

Alright folks, if you're feeling like freelancing is the way to go for you, then go for it! It's a great way to make some extra cash, or even turn it into a full-time gig. But remember, it's not just about finding a job and getting paid. It's about building a network, creating a portfolio, and constantly learning and improving your skills. So don't be afraid to put yourself out there, and start networking and bidding on projects today! And if you're a photographer looking for clients, give Upwork a try. With a little effort and patience, you'll be booking gigs in no time. Happy freelancing!

ppp

ELEVEN

DELIVERY EXECUTIVE

Do you have sudden cravings or procrastinate about cooking? Zomato or Swiggy would have saved you. Have you ever wondered who the people delivering to your door are? These are Delivery Executives assigned to pick up and deliver food, parcels, couriers, and other items from one location to another within a specific time frame. Implied is the responsibility to keep the allotted things safe and tight and verify the recipient's identity before delivering the package.

Meet John, a software engineer working for a tech company for the past 5 years. Despite his steady income, John has always looked for ways to supplement his earnings.

One day, he comes across an advertisement for a delivery executive for a popular food delivery service. Intrigued, John decides to give it a try.

At first, John sees it as a way to generate a little side income. However, as he begins to take on more deliveries, he realizes that he enjoys the freedom and independence the job provides. Not only does he get to be his own boss, but he also gets to explore different parts of the city and interact with various people.

John soon discovers that delivering food can be pretty lucrative, and he can earn a significant amount of money each month. He sticks with the job and starts prioritizing it over his day job.

As John becomes more experienced, he starts to develop a reputation as a reliable and efficient delivery executive. He receives positive customer feedback, and the food delivery service starts offering him exclusive bonuses and incentives.

John's secondary income as a delivery executive provides him with financial stability and a sense of fulfillment and purpose. He feels proud to have built a successful side hustle and enjoys the added income and freedom it provides.

Why?

You would also wonder about the benefits of being a delivery executive, as it offers flexibility in time and allows you to work in any part of the day you are free, whether day or night. The best part is that it is on your terms with a good salary, as this job offers low commitment and devotion. It also offers extra benefits, such as insurance borne by the company. Also, people have benefited from financial freedom, which is always a plus.

Due to startups coming in, options for work have increased. Now, not only Amazon and Flipkart need it, but also Zomato, Swiggy, Dunzo, Uber, Rapido, and Ola; everyone's base is logistics, which delivery executives create.

Steps-by-Step Guide

As soon as you decide to work as a delivery executive, you have options such as full-time, part-time, and temporary employment.

Verifying all government identification documents, such as AADHAR, PAN, and a driving license is mandatory. Some companies also check educational backgrounds, which is entirely dependent on them. Their minimum requirement is a high school diploma. Employers will assess your communication skills. A basic understanding of the English language is preferred. A minimal joining fee must be paid when starting, after which an online training course must be undertaken.

Suppose you wish to join Zomato as a delivery executive, and you can do it in the following easy-peasy steps-

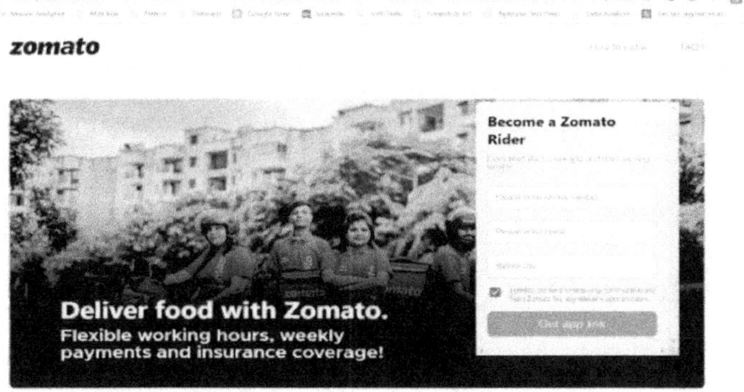

Step 1: Visit this website-https://www.zomato.com/deliver-food/

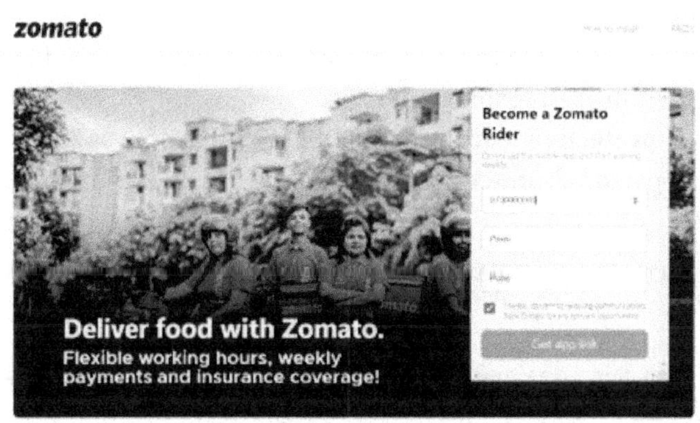

Step 2: Register with your details in the dialog box, as shown above. Find the "Become a Delivery Partner" or "Join as a Delivery Executive" section.

Step 3: Fill out the registration form with your personal and contact information, including your name, email address, phone number, and address.

Step 4: Complete the online traninig.

Step 5: Upload required documents, such as your ID proof, driving license, and vehicle registration papers (if you are using your own vehicle for deliveries).

Step 6: Complete a background check, which may include a verification of your personal information and driving record.

Step 7: Familiarize yourself with the app and the delivery process, and be prepared to start making deliveries. Start delivering and earning :)

Note: The exact steps and requirements for registering may vary slightly between Zomato and Swiggy, so it's essential to review each company's specific guidelines.

Cost-Benefit Analysis

Costs

1. **Vehicle expenses:** Delivery executives who use their own vehicles for deliveries will incur fuel, maintenance, and insurance costs.
2. **Phone and data plans:** Delivery executives will need a smartphone with a data plan to use the delivery app.
3. **Tax obligations:** Delivery executives are responsible for paying their own taxes, including self-employment taxes.
4. **Personal protective equipment:** Delivery executives may need to purchase personal protective equipment such as face masks and hand sanitizer.

Benefits

1. **Flexible schedule:** Delivery executives can choose their own hours and take time off when needed.
2. **Additional income:** Delivery executives can earn extra money in their spare time or make it a full-time job.
3. **Independence:** Delivery executives can work on their own terms without the constraints of a traditional 9-5 job.
4. **Opportunity to explore:** Delivery executives can explore different parts of the city and interact with various people.
5. **Potential bonuses and incentives:** Some delivery platforms offer bonuses and incentives for high-performing delivery executives.
6. **No prior experience required:** Delivery executives do not need prior experience or special skills to start.

Delivery executives need to weigh the costs and benefits before starting the job. The best decision for one individual may not be the same for another, so carefully consider your circumstances.

Your compensation from the business depends on the delivery distance. You are paid for the pickup and drop points, where you deliver the food to the client. For every delivery, the Zomato delivery boy receives at least 40 kilometers. You are entitled to additional compensation if the travel distance between the consumer and the restaurant exceeds 4.5 km. For every 1 km over 4.5 km, you receive an additional 10.

Skills Required

1. **Good time management:** Ability to plan and prioritize deliveries effectively to meet deadlines.
2. **Good communication skills:** Ability to communicate effectively with customers and other stakeholders.
3. **Navigation skills:** Ability to use maps and navigation tools to find the quickest and most efficient route to each delivery location.
4. **Physical fitness:** Ability to lift and carry heavy packages and navigate stairs, sidewalks, and another terrain while making deliveries.
5. **Attention to detail:** Ability to accurately follow delivery instructions and pay attention to details such as addresses and delivery instructions.
6. **Problem-solving skills:** Ability to think on your feet and find creative solutions to delivery challenges.
7. **Customer service skills:** Ability to handle customer inquiries and complaints in a professional and friendly manner.
8. **Responsiveness and reliability:** Ability to respond quickly to delivery requests and show up on time for each delivery.
9. **Driving skills:** Ability to drive safely and legally, with a valid license and insurance.

These skills can help increase a delivery executive's efficiency and effectiveness and increase the likelihood of success in the job.

Call-to-Action

You have the power to control your income and schedule by becoming a delivery executive. Take the first step and see where it takes you. Believe in yourself and give it a try. Everyone brings you closer to financial freedom.

In conclusion, being a delivery executive offers flexibility in terms of time, a good salary, and additional benefits such as insurance. Startups like Zomato, Swiggy, Dunzo, Uber, Rapido, and Ola are constantly hiring delivery executives, and the job requires minimal qualifications and government identification documents.

ÞÞÞ

TWELVE

NETWORK MARKETING

I am a person who loves to socialize and connect with people from different backgrounds and professions. Converting strangers into friends is a challenging task for me. If this is relatable for you, continue reading.

Network marketing relies on direct sales by independent agents, who frequently operate from their homes. For a network marketing organization, you should establish a network of business partners or salespeople to assist with client acquisition and transaction completion.

Businesses that use the network marketing model frequently organize salespeople into tiers, i.e., they are urged to build their networks of salespeople. The creator of a new deck receives a commission on their sales and the sales of the individuals in the level they created. Over time, a new story may give rise to yet another tier, increasing both the middle and top tier's commissions.

As a result, product sales and recruitment affect salespeople's wages—people who entered first and are in the top tier profit the most.

Here is a list of some well-known network marketing companies in India:

1. Amway India
2. Herbalife India
3. Tupperware India
4. Oriflame India
5. Avon India
6. Modicare
7. Vestige
8. Unicity India
9. Forever Living Products India

10. Mi Lifestyle Marketing Global Pvt Ltd

Why?

Network marketing, also known as multi-level marketing, is a business model that allows individuals to become independent distributors and earn income by promoting and selling products or services to a network of customers. While some people may have negative perceptions of network marketing, it can be a viable and lucrative option for those who are willing to put in the effort and have a passion for entrepreneurship.

- **Influence:** Your opinions can shape the development and improvement of products and services.
- **Flexibility:** You can work from anywhere and choose your schedule.
- **Low start-up cost:** Most network marketing businesses have a low start-up cost compared to traditional companies.
- **Unlimited income potential:** Your earning potential is based on your effort and the size of your network rather than a salary cap.
- **Personal development:** Network marketing often emphasizes personal growth and development through training and mentorship opportunities.
- **Network support:** You have the support of a team, including mentors and peers, to help you reach your goals.

Steps to Start

Starting a network marketing business can be an exciting and fulfilling career choice for those who are willing to put in the time and effort to build a successful business. Like any business, it requires careful planning and execution to ensure success. In this guide, we will outline the key steps involved in starting a network marketing business, from identifying the right opportunity to building a strong team and growing your customer base. Whether you are new to the world of network marketing or have experience in the industry, these steps will help you build a solid foundation for your business and achieve your goals.

1. **Research**: Research the company and products, and familiarize yourself with the compensation plan and business opportunity.
2. **Sign up**: Complete the online application or contact an Amway Independent Business Owner (IBO) to sign up as an IBO.
3. **Training**: Attend training sessions provided by the company or an experienced IBO to learn about the products, sales, and marketing techniques.
4. **Build your team**: Recruit and mentor new IBOs to build your team and increase your earning potential.
5. **Start selling**: Start selling the products by promoting them to your friends, family, and network.
6. **Follow up**: Follow up with your customers to ensure their satisfaction and to build long-term relationships.
7. **Attend events**: Attend local and national events hosted by Amway to network with other IBOs and learn new skills.
8. **Stay organized**: Keep track of your sales, expenses, and team members, and follow the company's rules and regulations.
9. **Continuously educate yourself**: Stay informed about the latest products, trends, and marketing strategies to improve your performance.

Starting a network marketing business with Amway or any other company requires time, effort, and commitment. The success of your business will depend on your sales and marketing skills, your team-building abilities, and your persistence.

Cost-Benefit Analysis

When considering whether to pursue network marketing, it's important to weigh the costs and benefits. The costs include start-up fees, marketing expenses, and inventory costs. On the other hand, the benefits are numerous and include flexibility, unlimited income potential, low overhead, personal and professional growth opportunities, tax deductions, more time with family and friends, and a sense of community. Unlike a traditional business, network marketing offers the flexibility to work from anywhere and set your own schedule, while also providing the potential for significant income based on your sales and effort. Additionally, the low overhead costs make it an attractive option for those seeking an entrepreneurial path with fewer financial risks. Overall, a cost benefit analysis of network marketing can help individuals determine if it's a viable and rewarding career choice.

Skills Required

Building a successful network marketing business requires a combination of entrepreneurial skills and personal attributes. While anyone can start a network marketing business, those who are successful often possess certain key skills and qualities. In this guide, we will outline the essential skills and personal attributes needed to start and grow a successful network marketing business. From strong communication and sales skills to persistence and a growth mindset, we'll cover everything you need to know to build a thriving network marketing business. Whether you're new to the industry or an experienced network marketer, these skills will help you lay a solid foundation for your business and achieve your goals.

1. **Communication:** Network marketers must communicate effectively with potential customers and business partners in person and through digital channels.
2. **Sales Network:** Marketers must be able to sell products and convince others to join the business.
3. **Leadership:** Network marketers must be able to inspire and motivate their teams to achieve success.
4. **Organization:** Network marketers must be able to manage their time and resources effectively, as well as keep track of their sales and customer information.
5. **Adaptability:** Network marketing involves constantly changing products, promotions, and business models, so network marketers must adapt to new circumstances and learn new skills quickly.
6. **Networking:** Network marketers must be able to build and maintain relationships with their customers and partners and expand their network to reach new customers.
7. **Passion:** Network marketers must have a genuine interest in the products they sell and the opportunity to help others achieve financial success.
8. **Resilience:** Network marketing can be challenging, and network marketers must persevere through setbacks and rejections and maintain a positive attitude.

Call-to-Action

There once was a young fellow by the name of Anubhav. He was a hardworking individual but struggled to make ends meet with just her full-time job as a teacher. Despite working long hours, he still couldn't save enough money for his future.

One day, a friend Abhishek told him about network marketing, a way to earn extra income by selling products and recruiting others to do the same. Anubhav was hesitant initially, but he was in dire need of additional income. He started by selling products to his friends and family, and he was surprised at how well they did. Anubhav earned a few hundred dollars each month, which significantly impacted his life.

As Anubhav's network of customers and sales associates grew, so did his income. He was able to work part-time hours while earning a full-time income. He was amazed at how much he could save and invest in his future while doing something he enjoyed.

His success in network marketing inspired her to help others do the same. He started to mentor and train others on building their network marketing businesses. Many of them went on to achieve great success as well.

Years later, Anubhav could retire early and live comfortably, all thanks to his decision to try network marketing as a secondary source of income. He was proud of the life he built for himself and the lives he helped change for others.

With the ability to expand your network and earn commissions from the sales of those in your network, the potential for growth and financial success is limitless. Be brave, take the first step, and start building your network today. Remember, success comes from hard work, dedication, and persistence. So, stay motivated, stay focused, and don't give up on your dreams; the effort you put in today will pay off in the future. Do you aim to become next Sarah?

Concluding, network marketing is a business model that relies on direct sales by independent agents and the building of a network of business partners or salespeople to assist with client acquisition and transaction completion. Businesses that use network marketing typically organize salespeople into tiers, with those who entered first and are in the top tier benefitting the most.

ೲೲೲ

THIRTEEN
PAID ONLINE SURVEY

I used to ponder if I could make money from the comfort of my own home with little or no time commitment and do it when I was free and in the mood. I'm sure you would somewhere as well. Continue reading because I found it.

A paid online survey is a type of market research where individuals are compensated for completing a survey questionnaire. Companies and market research firms use paid online surveys to gather information about consumer preferences, opinions, and behavior. The surveys are typically conducted over the internet and can be completed on a computer, tablet, or smartphone. Participants are usually offered a cash incentive or other rewards for completing the survey. Paid online surveys provide a convenient way for individuals to earn some extra income while also contributing to market research.

Online surveys are a method of gathering information about people's opinions on a specific topic. Organizations use it to understand the market better, change trends, analyze problems, gather product feedback, achieve customer satisfaction, and even gather feedback before launching a new product. You can earn money by being the respondent. You have to say what you know and what you think. SIMPLE, SORTED. This one is best for introverts.

Why?

Here are some reasons why individuals may choose to earn money through paid online surveys:

1. **Convenience**: Paid online surveys can be completed from the comfort of your own home, at any time, and from any device with internet access.
2. **Flexibility**: Participants can choose the surveys they wish to complete and set their own schedule for completing them.
3. **Extra income**: Paid online surveys can provide a source of extra income, allowing individuals to earn some extra cash in their spare time.
4. **No experience required**: Paid online surveys do not require any special skills or qualifications, making them accessible to a wide range of individuals.
5. **Easy to start**: Participating in paid online surveys is simple and straightforward, with no complicated application process or long-term commitment.
6. **Opinion matters**: Paid online surveys allow individuals to voice their opinions and have an impact on the products and services they use.

Here are some platforms that offer paid online surveys in India:

1. **Google Rewards:** It is a program offered by Google that rewards users for taking part in surveys and research studies.
2. **Survey Junkie:** A market research company that pays participants for completing online surveys.
3. **Swagbucks:** A rewards platform that offers cash and gift card incentives for completing online surveys, watching videos, and shopping online.
4. **Toluna:** A market research platform that pays participants for completing online surveys, testing products, and sharing opinions.
5. **InboxDollars:** A platform that pays participants for completing online surveys, watching videos, playing games, and shopping online.
6. **Vindale Research:** A market research company that pays participants for completing online surveys, reading emails, and referring friends.
7. **LifePoints:** A market research platform that pays participants for completing online surveys and participating in research studies.
8. **iPoll:** A market research platform that pays participants for completing online surveys, testing products, and participating in focus groups.
9. **SurveyClub:** A platform that connects participants with market research companies looking for participants for online surveys and focus groups.

It is important to thoroughly research and compare the reputation, payment terms, and privacy policies of each platform before signing up to participate in paid online surveys.

Steps to Start

Step 1: Enroll in online surveys for different brands. Enter your basic details. Usually, companies launch their online surveys every two weeks or once each month.

I will walk you through how we can use **Google Reward**'s procedure. The program is available through the Google Opinion Rewards app, which is available for download on the Google Play Store. Users can earn rewards, such as Google Play credit, by completing short surveys on various topics, such as their opinion on advertising or the latest products. The surveys are quick and easy to complete and are available on a first-come, first-served basis. The rewards earned through the program can be redeemed for purchasing items on the Google Play Store, such as apps, games, movies, and more. It is important to note that Google Rewards is only available in select countries and may not be available in all regions.

Step 1: Go to **https://surveys.google.com/google-opinion-rewards/** and download their app.

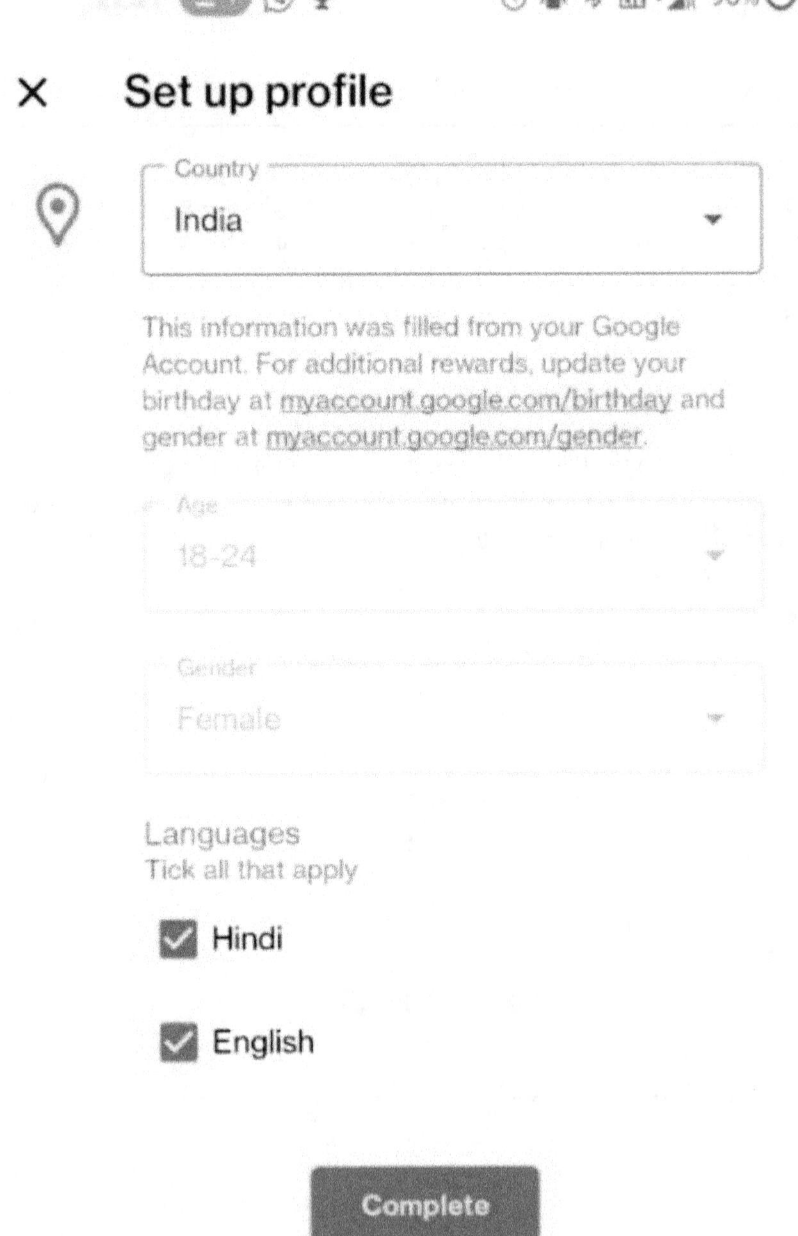

Step 2: Login and Setup as Directed

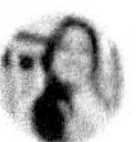

Google Opinion Rewards

GOOGLE PLAY BALANCE

₹0.00

 Play Store

MY TASKS

New survey available!
Expires in 23 hours.

Answer Survey

Share with your friends

Share the Google Opinion Rewards
app with your friends so they can start
earning too.

Share now

Step 3: Notification of New Survey

Step 4: Start earning :)

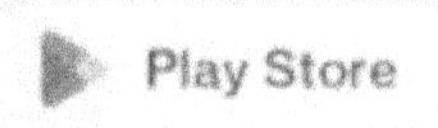

Payment Received

To summarise, here are the basic steps and guidelines for the same-

1. **Research:** Research various survey websites and read reviews from other users to find reputable and high-paying options.
2. **Sign up:** Create an account on the survey websites chosen and complete any necessary profile information.
3. **Keep track:** Organize the websites used, which surveys have been completed, and the rewards received.

4. **Be selective:** Prioritize surveys that offer higher rewards and have a shorter time commitment.

5. **Complete surveys:** Participate in available surveys and answer questions truthfully and accurately.

6. **Cash out:** Once the required minimum amount has been earned, cash out the rewards through the chosen payment method (e.g., PayPal).

7. **Repeat:** Continuously participate in surveys to maximize earnings and supplement income.

Cost-Benefit Analysis

Answering a survey questionnaire typically takes 3-5 minutes, which can earn you 80–150 rupees.

Costs

- **Time**: Completing online surveys takes time, and not all surveys will be available or provide rewards.
- **Limited earning potential**: The pay for online surveys is often low, and the number of surveys available may be limited.
- **No guarantee of qualification:** Not all surveys will qualify for rewards, which can waste time.

Benefits

- **Convenience**: Paid online surveys can be completed from the comfort of your own home, at any time, and from any device with internet access.
- **Flexibility**: Participants can choose the surveys they wish to complete and set their own schedule for completing them.
- **Extra income**: Paid online surveys can provide a source of extra income, allowing individuals to earn some extra cash in their spare time.
- **No experience required**: Paid online surveys do not require any special skills or qualifications, making them accessible to a wide range of individuals.
- **Easy to start**: Participating in paid online surveys is simple and straightforward, with no complicated application process or long-term commitment.

The potential benefits of participating in paid online surveys as a secondary income include convenience and flexibility. In contrast, the costs include time commitment and limited earning potential. Ultimately, the cost-benefit analysis will depend on the individual's goals and expectations

Skills Required

The skills required to attempt a paid online survey as a secondary income are:

1. **Attention to detail:** To ensure the accuracy of responses and maximize earnings, it's essential to pay attention to each question and answer it thoroughly.
2. **Good comprehension:** Understanding the questions and their context is essential to give meaningful answers.
3. **Time management:** Surveys can take minutes to an hour to complete, so managing time effectively is essential.
4. **Patience:** Not all surveys will be available, and not all will qualify for rewards, so patience and persistence are essential.
5. **Technology skills:** Familiarity with using computers and internet browsers is necessary to complete online surveys.
6. **Critical thinking:** Some surveys may require evaluating products or services, and having the ability to think critically and form opinions is essential.
7. **Organization:** Keeping track of the surveys and earnings received can help maximize profits and streamline the process.

Pro Tip: Provide truthful responses to get compensated. You can't sign up for every online survey. Some companies inquire about you and then connect you with a study that fits your profile.

Call-to-Action

Once upon a time, a person named Bhavna was looking for ways to supplement his income. He found an ad for paid online surveys and decided to try them.

Bhavna signed up for multiple survey websites and completed surveys in his spare time. At first, she was excited about the potential to make money from the comfort of his own home. However, she soon realized that the pay was not as high as he expected and the number of surveys available was limited. Despite these setbacks, John continued to complete surveys whenever they became available. She found that combining multiple websites could earn a small amount of extra cash each month.

One day, Bhavna came across a survey that promised a large reward for completing it. Excited by the prospect of earning a significant sum, he dedicated a whole day to completing the survey. However, after several hours of answering questions, she was informed that he did not qualify for the reward.

Frustrated but determined, Bhavna continued to take surveys. She learned to be more selective about her surveys and prioritize those that offered the highest rewards. Over time, she increased his earnings and made a noticeable difference in his monthly income.

Her experience with paid online surveys taught her that while they may not be a reliable source of income, they can provide a helpful boost to her finances. She continued to take surveys whenever she could, always searching for new and better opportunities to supplement her income.

A fantastic method to start making extra money while working from home is to start taking paid online surveys. Remember that every survey you complete is a step closer to making money, so be encouraged if you don't qualify for every survey. Keep at it, and you'll be able to earn a steady income in no time. So don't wait any longer. Take the first step today and earn money by participating in online surveys.

In conclusion, online surveys are a way for organizations to gather information about people's opinions on a specific topic, and for individuals to earn money by participating as a respondent. The process is simple and requires little time commitment, making it a suitable option for people who want to make money from the comfort of their own home. No qualifications are necessary to participate in online surveys.

ϷϷϷ

FOURTEEN

GET PAID WITH ANSWER QUESTIONS

Imagine a person named Sarah who is a stay-at-home mom and is looking for ways to make some extra money. One day, she came across a website called "Get Paid With Answer Questions" which promises to pay people for answering questions on various topics. Sarah decided to give it a try and signed up for an account.

The first thing she noticed was that the website offered a variety of topics to choose from, such as sports, technology, and entertainment. Sarah was excited to see that she could answer questions on topics she was knowledgeable about and get paid for it.

She started by answering a few easy questions on sports and was surprised to see that she was paid $0.50 for each correct answer. The more she answered, the more she earned, and she soon realized that she could make a decent amount of money by participating in this program.

Over the next few weeks, Sarah answered questions on a variety of topics and was able to make an extra $100. She was pleased with the extra money she was able to earn and was able to use it to buy some much-needed items for her family.

In conclusion, Sarah's experience with "Get Paid With Answer Questions" was positive and she was able to earn some extra money while using her knowledge and skills. This program allowed her to earn money on her own terms and at her own pace. If you're looking for a way to make some extra money, consider participating in a program like this, where you can get paid to answer questions and use your knowledge and skills to earn money.

There are many websites and platforms that allow individuals to get paid for answering questions. Here are some of the most popular ones:

1. **JustAnswer**: A platform where experts can answer questions on a wide range of topics and get paid for their expertise.
2. **Quora Partner Program**: A program on the Quora platform that allows users to earn money by answering questions and writing high-quality content.
3. **ChaCha**: A platform that pays individuals to answer questions via text message and provide information on a wide range of topics.
4. **PrestoExperts**: A platform that connects individuals with experts who can answer questions and provide advice on a wide range of topics.
5. **KnowledgeNuts**: A platform that pays individuals to answer trivia questions and provide information on a wide range of topics.
6. **Wonder**: A platform that allows individuals to earn money by conducting online research and answering questions for clients.

The amount of money you can earn by answering questions will vary depending on the platform and the type of questions you are answering. It is important to research the reputation, payment terms, and privacy policies of each platform before signing up to participate.

Why?

Using programs like "Get Paid With Answer Questions" to generate income has several benefits, including:

- **Flexibility**: You can participate in this program at any time and from any location, as long as you have an internet connection. This makes it an ideal option for individuals who have a busy schedule or who prefer to work from home.
- **No prior experience required**: Participating in this program does not require any specific skills or qualifications, making it accessible to a wide range of individuals.
- **Potential to earn extra income**: Depending on how much time and effort you put into answering questions, you can earn a significant amount of extra income.

- **Fun and interesting**: Participating in this program can be an enjoyable and interesting experience, as you can answer questions on topics you are knowledgeable about and get paid for it.
- **Opportunity to improve knowledge**: Answering questions on a variety of topics can help you improve your knowledge and keep your mind active.
- **Low risk**: Participating in this program has low risk, as there is no investment required and you only get paid for correct answers.

In conclusion, using programs like "Get Paid With Answer Questions" to generate income can be a flexible, accessible, and low-risk way to earn extra income while having fun and improving your knowledge.

Steps to Start

Here's a step by step guide on how to make money through the **Quora Partner Program**:

- **Create a Quora account**: The first step is to create a Quora account and establish yourself as an active user by asking and answering questions on a variety of topics.
- **Apply to the Quora Partner Program**: Once you have established yourself as an active user, you can apply to the Quora Partner Program. You will need to provide some basic information about yourself and your experience with Quora.
- **Wait for approval**: Once you have applied, Quora will review your application and approve you for the program if you meet their eligibility criteria.
- **Choose topics to write about**: After being approved, you can choose topics to write about and start answering questions on those topics.
- **Monetize your answers**: Quora will monetize your answers by displaying ads alongside them. You will earn money based on the number of views your answers receive and the number of clicks on the ads.
- **Track your earnings**: You can track your earnings through the Quora Partner Program dashboard.
- **Optimize your answers**: To maximize your earnings, it is important to write high-quality answers that provide value to readers and are

optimized for search engines.

- **Consistently participate**: Consistently participating in the Quora Partner Program by answering questions on a regular basis is important to ensure that you continue to earn money.

Here's a link to the Quora Partner Program website for more information: **https://www.quora.com/partners**

Note: Information on this website is subject to change, so it's always a good idea to check the site directly for the most up-to-date information.

Cost-Benefit Analysis

The cost-benefit analysis of the Quora Partner Program involves weighing the potential benefits of making money by answering questions against any costs or drawbacks associated with participating in the program.

Benefits

- **Flexibility**: The Quora Partner Program allows you to earn money on your own schedule and from the comfort of your own home.
- **Knowledge sharing**: By answering questions on topics you are knowledgeable about, you can share your expertise with others and help them find the information they need.
- **Passive income**: Once you have answered questions, you will continue to earn money as long as your answers receive views and clicks.
- **Low startup cost**: Participating in the Quora Partner Program does not require a large initial investment, making it a low-risk way to earn money.

Drawbacks

- **Time investment**: Writing high-quality answers takes time, and you may need to invest a significant amount of time to see results.
- **Competition**: There may be a lot of competition in certain niches, making it more difficult to earn money in those areas.
- **Uncertainty**: Your earnings will depend on the number of views and clicks your answers receive, and there is no guarantee that you will make a certain amount of money.

In conclusion, the Quora Partner Program can be a good way to earn money for those who have the time and knowledge to write high-quality answers on topics they are knowledgeable about. However, it is important to consider both the benefits and drawbacks before participating in the program to ensure that it is a good fit for your needs and goals.

Skills Required

The skills required to participate in the Quora Partner Program include:

- **Writing ability**: You will need to be able to write clear, concise, and well-researched answers to questions on topics you are knowledgeable about.
- **Knowledge in a particular area**: You will need to be knowledgeable about the topics you write about in order to provide valuable answers to users.
- **Attention to detail**: You will need to pay close attention to the questions you are answering and ensure that your answers are accurate and complete.
- **Marketing skills**: To maximize your earnings, you may need to have some basic marketing skills, such as understanding how to optimize your answers for search engines and promote your answers to get more views and clicks.
- **Patience**: Earning money through the Quora Partner Program takes time, and you may need to be patient and persistent in order to see results.

Call-to-Action

If you have a passion for sharing your knowledge and the skills required to participate in the Quora Partner Program, then now is the time to turn your expertise into income! With the flexibility to work on your own schedule, the opportunity to share your knowledge with others, and the potential to earn passive income, the Quora Partner Program is a great way to monetize your skills. Whether you are looking to supplement your current income or build a new source of income, the Quora Partner Program is a low-risk, high-reward opportunity that you can start today. So, why wait? Sign up for the Quora Partner Program and start earning money by answering questions on topics you are knowledgeable about!

ৡৡৡ

FIFTEEN

AFFILIATE MARKETING

Hey there! So, you want to know what affiliate marketing is? Well, imagine you have a friend who is always talking about the latest and greatest products. And every time someone asks your friend where they got that cool new gadget or how they discovered that amazing new service, they give them a little referral link.

And then, every time someone clicks on that link and buys something, your friend gets a little commission for it. That's affiliate marketing in a nutshell!

It's like having a side hustle without actually having to sell anything yourself. You just promote products you love and when people buy them through your unique link, you get a piece of the pie. It's like being a matchmaker for products and customers!

It's a win-win situation, really. The customer gets to discover a new product they might not have found otherwise, and you get a little something for your effort. It's like getting paid for playing Cupid.

So, that's affiliate marketing, folks! It's easy, it's fun, and it can be a great way to earn a little extra cash. So, why not give it a shot and start earning some dough for spreading the love!

Why?

Affiliate marketing is a great choice for those who want to start an online business or earn additional income. One of the key benefits of affiliate marketing is that it requires minimal start-up costs and you can work from anywhere with an internet connection. You don't need to create a product or worry about shipping, customer service, and other logistical issues that come with traditional businesses. As an affiliate marketer, you are promoting other people's products and earning a commission on each sale you make. This means you have the potential to earn a substantial income with a small investment of time and effort. Additionally, there is no limit to the number of products you can promote, giving you the opportunity to diversify your income streams. There is little cost and risk with fewer resources, little time and effort, and no commitment. Affiliate marketing enables businesses to sell products successfully while ensuring a high return on investment, increased brand recognition, and business expansion. Also, you can be an affiliate for multiple companies simultaneously. Work from anywhere.

AFFILIATE MARKETING STATS

80% of brands and **84%** of publishers use affiliate marketing.

Approximately **15%** of the digital media industry's revenue now comes from affiliate marketing.

Affiliate marketing generates **16%** of all e-commerce sales in the US and Canada.

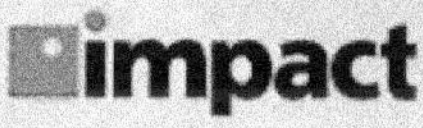

Source
Rakuten Advertising, Business Insider

Affiliate Marketing Statistics

Steps to Start

Step 1- Choose a company.

    I will show you how to be an Amazon Affiliate Marketer.

    Go to **https://affiliate-program.amazon.in/.**

    Step 2- Sign Up

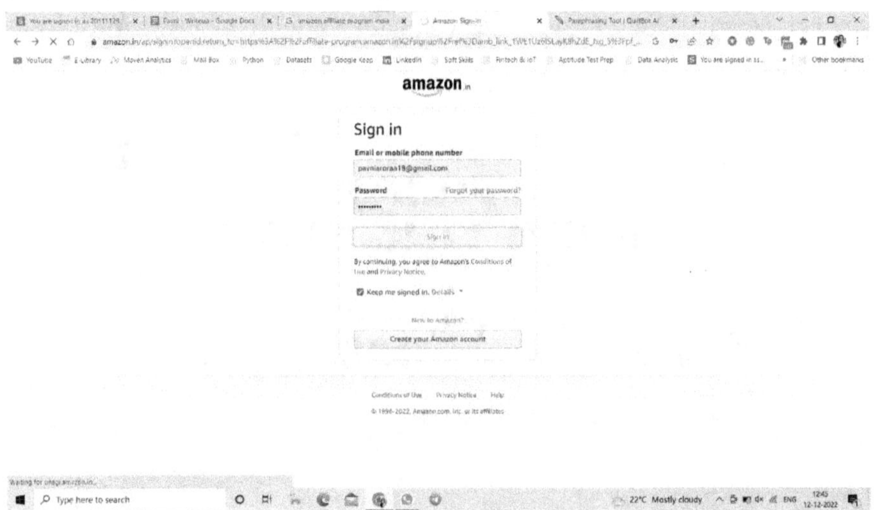

Sign Up Page

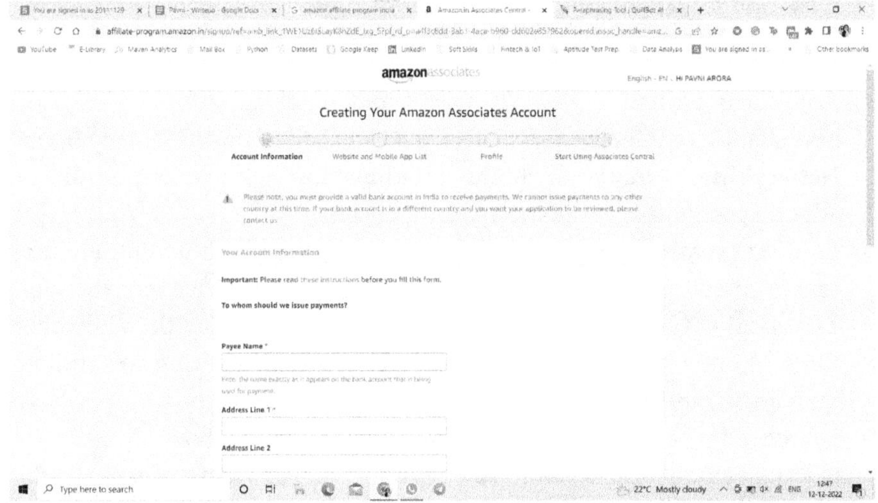

Registration Process

Step 3: After successfully signing up with all details, you can now recommend products through any means. Major publishers, individual bloggers, and social media influencers have developed specialized connecting tools.

Step 4: Through the traffic, you send to Amazon, you make money from qualified sales. Depending on the type of product purchased, different advertising fees apply.

Skills Required

Affiliate marketing is a popular and lucrative business model that allows individuals to earn money by promoting other people's products or services. It involves creating content, attracting an audience, and referring them to a company's product or service in exchange for a commission. While the potential for success is high, it's important to understand that affiliate marketing requires a particular set of skills to thrive. In this introduction, we will explore the key skills required to start an affiliate marketing business and provide insights into how you can acquire and develop them. By mastering these skills, you can position yourself to succeed in this competitive industry and achieve your financial goals.

- **Marketing and sales:** Understanding how to promote and sell products through various marketing channels, including email, social media, and content marketing.
- **Analytical skills:** Ability to track and analyze affiliate program performance and make data-driven decisions on optimizing campaigns.
- **Networking:** Ability to build relationships with other affiliates, advertisers, industry leaders, and influencers.
- **Content creation:** Ability to create engaging and high-quality content that promotes products, builds brand awareness, and drives conversions.
- **Technical skills:** Knowledge of website design, HTML, CSS, and other programming languages, as well as familiarity with tracking and affiliate management software.
- **Search engine optimization (SEO):** Understanding how to optimize website content and keywords for search engines to drive organic traffic to affiliate products.
- **Negotiation and communication:** Ability to effectively communicate and negotiate with advertisers to secure the best terms and commission rates.
- **Time management:** Ability to manage multiple affiliate campaigns and tasks while meeting deadlines and maintaining high productivity.

Cost-Benefit Analysis

Acquiring the necessary skills to start an affiliate marketing business can require an investment of both time and money. You may need to invest in training courses, online resources, and tools to improve your skills and knowledge. Additionally, it may take some time to see a return on your investment, especially if you're starting from scratch and need to build your audience and credibility.

The benefits of acquiring the skills required to start an affiliate marketing business are numerous. By investing in your education and development, you can gain the expertise and knowledge necessary to succeed in a competitive industry. This can lead to increased earning potential, as you'll be able to create more effective content and drive more traffic to your affiliate offers. Additionally, by building your skills, you can position yourself as an authority in your niche, which can help you attract and retain a loyal following. Finally, the skills you acquire in affiliate marketing can be applied to other areas of online marketing, making it a valuable investment for your career.

Call-to-Action

Once upon a time, there was a person named Aashruti who worked a 9-5 job as a software developer. Although he loved his job, he wanted to have a secondary source of income. One day, while browsing the internet, Aashruti came across the concept of affiliate marketing. She was fascinated by the idea of earning money by promoting products and decided to give it a try.

She started by researching and finding a niche that she was interested in, and found a company that offered an affiliate program for products related to that niche. She signed up for the program, and began promoting the products through her social media accounts and blog.

At first, Aashruti didn't see much success, but he didn't give up. She continued to learn more about affiliate marketing and read articles and watched videos on the subject. She also reached out to other successful affiliates for advice.

With time and effort, Aashruti's hard work paid off. She started to see a steady stream of commission from the sales of the products he was promoting. She was able to earn a few hundred dollars each month, which made a big difference in his financial situation.

She was thrilled with his success, and continued to grow his affiliate marketing business. She diversified his income streams by promoting a variety of products in different niches. She even quit his day job and became a full-time affiliate marketer, earning a comfortable living while working from home.

In the end, Aashruti was grateful for discovering affiliate marketing as a secondary source of income. She learned that with determination and hard work, anything is possible.

Starting as an affiliate marketer can be a great way to supplement your income and achieve financial freedom. Remember that you can turn your passion into a successful business with hard work, determination, and a willingness to learn. Feel free to experiment and take risks, as this is how you will grow and succeed. Stay focused on your goals, and don't let setbacks discourage you. Remember that starting small doesn't mean you can't dream big. The most successful affiliate marketers began just like you, with a single idea and a lot of ambition. Believe in yourself and achieve great things

In conclusion, affiliate marketing is a method of promotion where companies pay outside publications to direct customers to their goods and services, with the commission payment encouraging third-party affiliate publishers to advertise the business. It offers little cost and risk, with fewer resources, little time and effort, and no commitment. Businesses can sell products successfully while ensuring a high return on investment, increased brand recognition, and business expansion.

ᐅᐅᐅ

SIXTEEN
TUTORING

The education sector is continually expanding and is a crucial factor in the growth and development of a country. India, in particular, is witnessing numerous revisions and developments in its education system as part of the New Education Policy (NEP). The curriculum and pedagogy adopted in educational institutions offer ample opportunities for the growth of students and teachers. As per the NEP, students are classified into advanced learners, average learners, and slow learners based on their learning skills. Sometimes, educational institutions may not be able to cater to all students with what they need to achieve their career goals. In a country like India, where a majority of parents are willing to invest in their children's education expenses, the demand for private tutoring is high.

Before the COVID-19 pandemic, private tutoring was not very popular, and tutors faced restrictions due to geographical limitations. However, the pandemic has created new opportunities for online teaching and video calls, making it possible for students from anywhere in the world to learn from anywhere in the world.

In the current scenario, there are numerous opportunities to earn income from private tutoring. All one needs is a good level of knowledge in the subject they want to teach. While a teacher's knowledge about the subject was previously the main focus, nowadays, the presentation style and teaching approach are equally essential. Private tutoring can be conducted in two ways: live sessions or recorded videos. In online sessions, tutors can register students from across the globe and conduct classes at a suitable time. In the second option, tutors can share recorded videos on various online platforms such as YouTube or start their own website. The main advantage of this method is that it is accessible to everyone at any time.

Why?

There are several reasons why tutoring can be a good way to earn secondary income:

- **Flexibility**: Tutoring is a flexible job that can be done part-time, allowing you to schedule your sessions around your primary job, school, or other commitments.
- **High demand**: There is a high demand for tutoring, especially in subjects like math, science, and English. This means that you are likely to have a steady stream of students and can earn a decent amount of money.
- **Rewarding**: Tutoring can be a very rewarding job as you are helping students achieve their academic goals and improve their understanding of a subject. Seeing your students improve can be a great source of satisfaction.
- **Personal development**: Tutoring can also be a great way to improve your own knowledge and skills. Teaching a subject requires you to have a deep understanding of it, which can help you develop your own expertise.
- **Entrepreneurship**: Starting a tutoring business can also be a great way to develop your entrepreneurial skills, such as marketing, customer service, and financial management.

Overall, tutoring can be a fulfilling and lucrative secondary income stream that allows you to use your skills and help others while maintaining a flexible schedule.

Step-by-Step Guide

Let's assume that you've got a talent for art and craft and you want to earn some extra cash? Great idea! Here's how you can turn your skills into a secondary income:

- **Decide on your target audience**: Determine who you want to teach. This could be children, teenagers, adults or a mix of all three. Decide on your target audience, and think about the kinds of art and craft projects they might be interested in.

- **Choose a platform**: There are a variety of platforms you can use to promote your art and craft services. You could create a website or blog, use social media platforms like Facebook, Instagram or Pinterest to showcase your skills, or even use word-of-mouth to advertise your services.
- **Set your rates**: Decide how much you want to charge for your services. Take into account the cost of materials, your time, and your experience. Be sure to research what other art and craft tutors are charging in your area, so you can be competitive.
- **Create a portfolio**: Build a portfolio of your work to showcase your skills and experience. Include pictures of previous projects you've worked on, as well as any relevant qualifications or training you've received.
- **Create lesson plans**: Create lesson plans for your art and craft projects. Think about what supplies and equipment you'll need, how long the project will take, and how you'll guide your students through the process.
- **Promote your services**: Start promoting your art and craft services through your chosen platform. Share pictures of your work and lesson plans, and encourage potential customers to get in touch with you.
- **Build relationships**: Once you start getting students, build relationships with them by providing a positive learning experience. Ask for feedback and make adjustments to your lessons as needed.
- **Expand your services**: Once you've built a solid customer base, consider expanding your services. You could offer workshops or group classes, or even start selling your art and craft products.

And there you have it! With these steps, you can turn your art and craft skills into a secondary income stream. Good luck, and have fun!

Skills Required

To be an effective tutor, there are several skills that are important to have. Here are some skills required for tutoring:

- **Expertise in the subject matter**: As a tutor, you need to have a deep understanding of the subject you're teaching. This means that you should have a solid foundation of knowledge and be able to explain concepts clearly and concisely.

- **Communication skills**: Being able to communicate effectively is crucial as a tutor. You should be able to explain complex ideas in a way that is easy to understand, and be patient and encouraging when working with students.
- **Adaptability**: Every student is different, and as a tutor, you need to be able to adapt your teaching style to fit the needs of each individual student. This means being flexible and willing to adjust your approach as needed.
- **Time management**: Tutoring often involves working with multiple students and managing your own schedule. It's important to be able to manage your time effectively so that you can meet the needs of all your students while also managing your other responsibilities.
- **Patience**: Learning can be a challenging process, and it's important to be patient with your students as they work through difficult concepts. Being patient and understanding can help students feel more comfortable and confident in their ability to learn.
- **Creativity**: Sometimes, students need to be engaged in the subject matter in new and creative ways. As a tutor, you should be able to come up with fun and creative ways to teach and reinforce concepts.
- **Positive attitude**: A positive attitude can make a big difference in a student's ability to learn. By being positive and encouraging, you can help your students feel more confident and motivated to learn.

Overall, the most successful tutors are those who are knowledgeable, patient, adaptable, and able to communicate effectively with their students. By developing these skills, you can become a highly effective and sought-after tutor.

Cost-Benefit Analysis

Costs

- **Time commitment**: Tutoring can require a significant amount of time, both in preparing lesson plans and actually teaching. This can be challenging to balance with other commitments, such as school or work.
- **Dealing with difficult students**: Not every student will be a pleasure to work with, and it can be frustrating to deal with those who are unmotivated or uncooperative.

- **Financial investment**: Tutoring may require a financial investment in materials, such as textbooks or supplies.

Benefits

- **Additional income**: Tutoring can be a lucrative side hustle, providing extra income that can be used to pay bills or save for future goals.
- **Flexibility**: Many tutors are able to set their own hours and work around their other commitments, which can be especially beneficial for those with busy schedules.
- **Personal fulfillment**: Helping others learn and succeed can be incredibly rewarding and fulfilling, and can even lead to positive relationships with students and their families.
- **Skill development**: Tutoring can help you develop valuable skills such as communication, teaching, and organization.

Overall, while tutoring can require a significant time commitment and investment, the benefits can outweigh the costs in terms of financial gain, personal fulfillment, and skill development.

Call-to-Action

So, are you passionate about a particular subject or skill? Do you enjoy helping others learn and succeed? If so, it's time to put your talents to work and start tutoring! Not only can tutoring provide you with a flexible and lucrative side hustle, but it can also be incredibly fulfilling and rewarding. You have the opportunity to make a real difference in the lives of your students, while also developing valuable skills and building positive relationships. So don't wait any longer - take the first step towards becoming a tutor today. Your future students are waiting for you!

ᕙᕙᕙ

SEVENTEEN

APP DEVELOPMENT

In recent years, app development has emerged as a highly profitable industry due to the increasing popularity of smartphones and tablets, with over 2.7 billion smartphone users worldwide. The potential for generating revenue through app development is substantial, and there are various ways to do so, including selling the app, in-app advertising, subscriptions, sponsorships, in-app purchases, and the freemium model.

One approach to monetizing an app is to sell it, either by setting a one-time purchase price or by offering it for free with in-app purchases. While selling an app can generate significant revenue upfront, it may not be suitable for all types of apps since some users may not be willing to pay for an app.

Developers can also generate revenue through in-app advertising, where ads are integrated into the app, and revenue is earned through clicks or impressions. This method is suitable for apps with a large user base and high engagement, but it's crucial to ensure that the number of ads doesn't negatively impact the user experience.

Subscriptions are another method of generating income, where users pay a monthly or annual fee for access to premium content or services. This approach works well for apps that offer premium features, but it can be challenging to maintain a consistent subscriber base.

Developers can also earn revenue through sponsorships, where companies pay to have branded content featured within the app. This approach is suitable for apps that have a large user base and a specific target audience, but it's important to ensure that the sponsored content is relevant to the app's users and doesn't negatively impact the user experience.

In-app purchases offer users the ability to purchase virtual items or additional features, making it an effective way to generate revenue for games and other apps that offer virtual goods or services. However, it's essential to ensure that in-app purchases don't make the app unbalanced or pay-to-win.

Finally, the freemium model allows users to try a basic version of the app for free and then charge for more advanced features or virtual goods. This approach is suitable for a wide range of apps, but the app's basic version must provide enough value to justify the in-app purchases.

To create a sustainable and profitable app development business, the most successful developers typically use a combination of monetization strategies. By understanding the different options available, developers can choose the best approach for their app and generate revenue while maintaining a positive user experience.

Generating income through app development may seem difficult if you don't have the necessary skills or experience. However, there are some ways that you can get started with little to no coding experience.

For example, you can use app development platforms like Appy Pie or BuildFire, which provide easy-to-use drag and drop interfaces to create and customize your own apps. These platforms allow you to create basic apps without any coding knowledge, and even offer tutorials and support to help you get started.

Let's say you are a 10-year-old kid who loves playing games and has an idea for a simple game app. You could use an app development platform like Appy Pie to create your game app, without needing to know how to code. You could use the drag and drop interface to design the game, add graphics and sound effects, and then publish it to the app stores.

To generate income, you could use in-app advertising as a monetization strategy. This means that you can integrate ads into your game app and earn revenue from clicks or impressions. For example, you could show a banner ad at the bottom of the screen or offer a reward video ad that users can watch to earn extra points or in-game currency.

By using an app development platform and monetizing your app with in-app advertising, you could generate income from your game app without needing any advanced coding skills. Of course, creating a successful app takes time, effort, and creativity, but it's possible to get started with simple tools and strategies.

Why Should You Consider Developing an App?

There are many reasons why someone might choose to develop an app. Here are some of the most common reasons:

- **Solving a problem**: Many successful apps are created to solve a specific problem or address a particular need. For example, a transportation app like Uber was developed to make it easier for people to get around, while a productivity app like Evernote was developed to help people manage their notes and tasks more efficiently.
- **Offering a unique product or service**: Developing an app can be a way to offer a unique product or service that fills a gap in the market. For example, a language learning app like Duolingo offers a unique way to learn languages on-the-go.
- **Making money**: App development can be a lucrative business, with various monetization strategies available. As mentioned earlier, developers can earn money through in-app advertising, subscriptions, sponsorships, in-app purchases, and selling the app itself.
- **Expanding reach**: Developing an app can be a way to expand your reach and connect with customers in a new way. With over 2.7 billion smartphone users worldwide, developing an app can be a great way to reach a wider audience and engage with them more directly.
- **Staying competitive**: In today's digital age, having an app can be a way to stay competitive and keep up with your competitors. If your competitors have apps, developing an app of your own can be a way to level the playing field and offer your customers a comparable experience.

Overall, there are many good reasons to develop an app, from solving a problem to making money to staying competitive in the market. It's important to carefully consider your goals and objectives before embarking on an app development project.

Step-by-Step Guide

First, let's start with the idea for your app. Suppose you want to create an app that helps people find hostels or PGs in a university area. This is a great idea! The first thing you'll want to do is to think about what features your app will have. For example, you might want to include a map that shows the location of hostels or PGs, the prices, the amenities available, and so on.

Once you have a clear idea of what you want your app to do, it's time to create a mockup or prototype. A mockup is a visual representation of your app that shows how it will look and function. You can use a tool like Balsamiq or Figma to create your mockup. This step is important because it helps you visualize your app and make sure that it will work the way you want it to.

After you have your mockup, it's time to find a developer to create your app. There are many online platforms where you can find app developers, such as Upwork or Freelancer. Make sure to choose a developer who has experience creating apps similar to yours, and who has good reviews from previous clients.

The next step is to work with the developer to create your app. The developer will use programming languages like Java or Swift to write the code that makes your app work. During this process, you'll want to stay in touch with your developer to make sure that your app is being developed according to your specifications.

Once your app is complete, it's time to test it. You'll want to test your app on different devices to make sure that it works properly. You can also ask friends or family members to test your app and give you feedback.

Finally, it's time to launch your app. You can upload your app to the Apple App Store or Google Play Store, depending on which platform you developed it for. Make sure to create a description of your app that clearly explains what it does and what features it has.

That's a basic overview of how to develop an app. It can be a complex process, but with careful planning and the right team, you can create an app that helps people find the perfect hostel or PG in a university area. Good luck!

Once you have developed the hostel/PG finder app, you may want to monetize it to generate income. There are a few ways to do this:

- **Advertising**: You can display ads within the app and earn money based on clicks or impressions.
- **Affiliate marketing**: You can earn a commission by partnering with hostels/PGs and promoting their services within the app.
- **Paid listings**: You can charge hostels/PGs for featuring their properties at the top of the search results or in a featured section.

- **Premium features**: You can offer additional features, such as detailed property information, booking options, or user reviews, for a fee.
- **In-app purchases**: You can offer additional services or features within the app, such as booking assistance or personalized recommendations, for a fee.

Cost-Benefit Analysis

The cost of developing an app can vary widely depending on a number of factors, such as the complexity of the app, the features it includes, and the platform it's being developed for. Here are some of the costs to consider when developing a hostel/PG finder app:

- **Development costs**: If you're not developing the app yourself, you will need to hire a developer or development team. The cost can range from a few thousand dollars to tens of thousands of dollars, depending on the complexity of the app and the experience of the developers.
- **Design costs**: You will need to hire a designer or design team to create the user interface and user experience of the app. The cost can range from a few hundred dollars to several thousand dollars.
- **Hosting costs**: Once your app is developed, you will need to host it on a server. Hosting costs can range from a few dollars a month to hundreds of dollars a month, depending on the server you choose.
- **Maintenance costs**: You will need to update and maintain the app to ensure it continues to work properly. Maintenance costs can range from a few hundred dollars a month to several thousand dollars a year, depending on the complexity of the app and the frequency of updates.

As for the benefits of developing a hostel/PG finder app, there are several:

- **A growing market**: The student housing market is growing, and there is a need for a convenient and reliable way to find hostels/PGs in university areas.
- **Revenue generation**: The app can be monetized in a number of ways, such as advertising, affiliate marketing, and in-app purchases.
- **Improved user experience**: The app can make it easier for students to find suitable housing options, saving them time and effort.

- **Competitive advantage**: A hostel/PG finder app can give you a competitive advantage over other companies in the student housing market.
- **Insights and data**: The app can provide valuable insights and data on user preferences, search patterns, and housing market trends, which can be used to improve the app and inform business decisions.

Overall, the cost and benefits of developing a hostel/PG finder app will depend on a number of factors. However, if done well, it has the potential to be a valuable and profitable addition to the student housing market.

The cost of developing an app can vary greatly depending on many factors, such as the complexity of the app, the features and functionality included, the platforms it will be available on, the location and rates of the developers involved, and any additional expenses related to marketing, testing, and maintenance.

For an app like the one described, the cost could range from around 1.5 lakhs to 4 lakhs or more, depending on the specifics. This includes costs such as the developer's fees, server costs, third-party API integration fees, and any other expenses associated with app development.

However, it's worth noting that the benefits of developing a successful app can far outweigh the costs. In addition to the potential for generating revenue through in-app purchases or advertisements, an app can also help to build a brand, increase visibility, and improve customer engagement and loyalty. It can also provide valuable data and insights on user behavior, preferences, and trends, which can be used to improve the app and inform business decisions.

Here's a table to help break down the potential costs involved in developing an app like the one described:

Cost Item	Estimated Cost (INR)
Developer fees	75,000 - 2,00,000
Server costs	10,000 - 25,000
Third-party API integration	5,000 - 15,000
Design and graphics	15,000 - 50,000
Testing and bug fixing	20,000 - 40,000
Marketing and promotion	15,000 - 50,000
Miscellaneous expenses	10,000 - 20,000
Total Estimated Cost	**1,50,000 - 4,00,000+**

Breakdown of Cost of Developing an App

Please note that these costs are only estimates and can vary depending on a number of factors, including the location and rates of the developers and service providers, the complexity of the app, the platforms it will be available on, and any additional features or functionality that are added during the development process.

Skills Required

Developing a mobile app can be a complex process, and typically requires a range of skills in order to bring the app to life. Some of the key skills required to develop a mobile app like the one described could include:

- **Programming skills**: Mobile app development typically requires proficiency in a programming language like Java, Swift, or Kotlin.
- **Mobile app development skills**: This includes knowledge of different mobile platforms and the tools and frameworks required to develop mobile apps.
- **User interface (UI) and user experience (UX) design**: A good app needs to be visually appealing and easy to use, which requires design skills to create a seamless user experience.

- **Database management**: The app may need to store user data, so knowledge of database management systems like MySQL or MongoDB may be necessary.
- **Server management**: Depending on the app's functionality, it may need to connect to servers to perform certain tasks, which requires knowledge of server management and backend development.
- **Testing and debugging**: Testing and debugging are critical to ensuring that the app functions properly and is free of errors.

While it is possible to learn these skills on your own, it can take time and effort to become proficient in all of these areas. Some people may choose to hire a team of developers with different skill sets to create an app, or they may work with freelancers or an app development agency to bring their app to life.

Call-to-Action

If you're interested in developing apps, don't be discouraged by the potential challenges. With the right mindset and resources, you can turn your app idea into a reality. There are plenty of tools and online resources available to help you learn the necessary skills and get started with app development.

Remember, the world is constantly evolving and technology is advancing at a rapid pace. There has never been a better time to become an app developer and make your mark on the world. So, if you have an idea that you're passionate about, take the first step and start exploring the world of app development today. Who knows? Your app could be the next big thing!

ᐅᐅᐅ

EIGHTEEN
WEBSITE CREATION

You are meeting your friend who launched his website to help people plan their travels one year ago. As a newbie in the website development world, you are curious to know how he conceptualized and developed the website, and how he is making money out of it. You are eager to learn from his experience, but knowing your friend's sense of humor, you can also expect some funny and sarcastic comments along the way.

- **You**: Hey man, how's it going? I heard you launched a travel website last year, that's dope!
- **Friend**: Thanks dude, it's been a wild ride. I've learned so much about building and running a website.
- **You**: That's sick bro. How did you even get started?
- **Friend**: Well, I just had this idea of creating a website that would help people plan their travel. I did a lot of research on the best website building platforms and settled on one that fit my budget.
- **You**: Damn, sounds complicated. How much did it cost you to build the website?
- **Friend**: It wasn't too bad actually. I used a free website builder and paid for some premium features that helped me optimize my website for search engines. All in all, it cost me about 10K.
- **You**: 10K?! That's hella expensive! Did you even make any money off of it?
- **Friend**: Oh yeah, definitely. I monetized my website by selling advertising space, and I also created some premium travel planning services that people can pay for. It's been a great source of income for me.
- **You**: That's lit! I might have to get in on this website building game. Any tips for a newbie like me?

- **Friend**: Just start with a simple idea and do your research. There's a lot of information out there, but if you're patient and persistent, you can definitely make it work. And don't be afraid to take risks and make mistakes - that's how you learn and grow.
- **You**: Got it, man. Thanks for the advice. I'm gonna start brainstorming some website ideas right now.
- **Friend**: Awesome, can't wait to see what you come up with. And hey, if you need any help or advice, just hit me up. We're in this website building game together, man!

In conclusion, developing a website can be a great way to share your passion with the world and make some extra cash. Whether you're into travel, fashion, cooking, or any other hobby, there's always a way to monetize your website and turn your passion into profit. So don't be afraid to give it a shot, keep learning and experimenting, and most importantly, have fun with it! Who knows, maybe in a year or two, you'll be the one telling me about your successful website and how you're living the dream.

If you're a newbie interested in website making, there are plenty of ideas to explore. Whether you want to create a personal blog, a small business website, or an online store, there are options to suit a wide range of interests and skill levels. In this response, we'll provide some website making ideas that you can consider as a starting point for your own project. From simple and straightforward to more complex and technical, these ideas will give you a sense of the possibilities and help you get started on your website making journey.

1. **Personal blog**: You can create a personal blog where you can share your thoughts, ideas, experiences, and opinions on different topics that interest you.
2. **Niche blog**: You can create a niche blog that focuses on a specific topic such as health, fitness, technology, or cooking.
3. **Online portfolio**: If you're an artist, writer, photographer, or designer, you can create an online portfolio to showcase your work and attract potential clients.
4. **E-commerce website**: You can create an e-commerce website to sell products online. You can source products from different manufacturers or create your own products.

5. **Online directory**: You can create an online directory that lists businesses, services, and professionals in a specific industry or location.
6. **Job board**: You can create a job board where employers can post job openings, and job seekers can search and apply for jobs.
7. **Online course**: You can create an online course that teaches a specific skill or knowledge. You can create your own course or collaborate with other experts.
8. **Social network**: You can create a social network that connects people with similar interests or goals. You can create a niche social network or a broader one.
9. **Online community**: You can create an online community where people can share ideas, support each other, and discuss common interests.
10. **Quiz or trivia website**: You can create a quiz or trivia website that tests people's knowledge on a specific topic such as history, geography, or pop culture.

Why Create a Website?

In today's digital age, having a website is becoming increasingly important for businesses and individuals alike. It provides a platform to showcase your products, services, or personal brand to a global audience. Whether you're an entrepreneur looking to launch your business or an artist seeking to showcase your work, a website can help you reach a wider audience and establish credibility. In this digital age, having a website can also make it easier for people to find you and engage with you. In this sense, a website is like a digital business card or a virtual storefront. Let's take a look at some reasons why you should create a website.

Creating a website can also help you establish your brand or online presence, which is increasingly important in today's digital world. With so many people turning to the internet for information and services, having a website can make it easier for potential customers or clients to find you and learn about what you have to offer. Additionally, a website can help you build credibility and trust with your audience, by providing valuable information and showcasing your expertise in your field.

Moreover, a website can also be a great way to connect with like-minded people, share your interests or hobbies, and build a community around a particular topic or niche. You can use your website to share your thoughts and ideas, engage with your audience through comments or social media, and even collaborate with other creators or businesses.

Whether you're looking to start a business, establish a personal brand, or simply share your passion with the world, creating a website can be a powerful tool to help you achieve your goals. With so many website building platforms and resources available, it's never been easier to get started and bring your vision to life.

Step-by-Step Guide

So, you've got this great idea for a website, and you want to bring it to life. Awesome! Creating a website can be a lot of fun, but it can also be a bit daunting if you're new to the process. Don't worry though, we've got you covered. In this step-by-step guide, we're going to walk you through the process of creating a website, just like the one mentioned in the previous section.

Now, before we get started, let's get one thing straight: creating a website is not rocket science. It may seem a little overwhelming at first, but with a bit of patience and determination, anyone can do it. And the best part? You don't need to be a tech genius or have a ton of money to create a great website. There are plenty of free and low-cost options out there that make it easy for anyone to build a website from scratch. So, if you're ready to dive in, let's get started!

Great! Now that you have a better understanding of what a website is and why you should create one, let's dive into the steps to actually create your own travel planning website. Here is a step-by-step guide:

- **Step 1**: Choose a domain name and hosting provider The first step is to choose a domain name and a hosting provider. Your domain name should be unique, easy to remember, and relevant to your website's content. You can purchase a domain name from various domain registrars like GoDaddy, Namecheap, or Bluehost. Once you have a domain name, you need a hosting provider to store your website's files and make them accessible online. You can choose from free hosting services or paid ones like Bluehost, SiteGround, or HostGator.
- **Step 2**: Install WordPress Once you have your domain name and hosting, you'll need to install a content management system (CMS) like WordPress. It is free and one of the most popular CMS platforms,

allowing you to easily customize your website and add content. You can install WordPress from your hosting provider's control panel or manually through FTP.

- **Step 3**: Choose a travel theme Now, you need to choose a travel theme for your website. A theme is a pre-designed template that you can customize to fit your website's branding and layout. You can find a variety of travel themes in WordPress's theme directory, like Travel Way, Adventure Journal, or The Trip.
- **Step 4**: Customize your website Once you have chosen a theme, you can start customizing your website. You can add your logo, change the color scheme, and create pages like About Us, Contact Us, and Home. You can also install plugins to add functionality to your website, like a booking system, Google Maps integration, or social media sharing buttons.
- **Step 5**: Create content The most important part of your travel planning website is the content. You can create blog posts, travel guides, or listicles that are relevant to your target audience. Make sure your content is engaging and informative, and includes photos and videos to make it more visually appealing.
- **Step 6**: Monetize your website Finally, you can monetize your website in various ways, like advertising, affiliate marketing, sponsored content, or selling travel-related products like e-books, courses, or merchandise. You can use Google AdSense for advertising or join affiliate programs like Booking.com or TripAdvisor to earn commission on bookings made through your website.

While the steps mentioned above are for a basic website, you can always customize and add more features to your website as you grow and learn. Remember to keep your website updated and stay active on social media to attract more visitors and engage with your audience.

Good luck with your website, and don't forget to have fun with it!

Cost and Benefit of Website Creation

Yo, my friend! Are you thinking of creating a website? Let me tell you, it's a great idea, and there are definitely some costs and benefits you should consider before jumping in.

First things first, let's talk about the costs. Obviously, there's going to be some financial investment involved. You'll need to pay for a domain name, web hosting, and potentially web design services or templates. Depending on the complexity of your website, these costs can add up pretty quickly.

But don't let that scare you away! The benefits of having a website can be huge. For one, it can help establish your online presence and credibility. People will be able to find you more easily and learn more about what you do. Plus, it can be a great way to showcase your work or products and connect with potential customers or clients.

Having a website also gives you more control over your online image. Instead of relying on social media platforms, which can be unpredictable and subject to algorithm changes, you have complete control over how your website looks and what content is displayed. Plus, you can use analytics tools to track your website traffic and user behavior, which can help you optimize your content and strategy over time.

In short, creating a website definitely requires some upfront investment, but the long-term benefits can be well worth it. So go ahead and give it a shot - who knows, it might be the best thing you ever do for your business or personal brand!

Skills Required

To create a successful website, there are a variety of skills that can be helpful to have. Firstly, a basic knowledge of coding languages such as HTML, CSS and JavaScript is necessary to develop and maintain a website. Additionally, having a good eye for design and aesthetics is important to create an attractive and user-friendly interface. A strong understanding of SEO (Search Engine Optimization) is also important to ensure that the website ranks well in search engines and drives traffic. It's important to be able to write engaging and informative content, and have good communication skills to effectively engage with website visitors and potential customers. Lastly, having a strong understanding of website analytics can help you to track website performance and optimize it over time. These skills are not all necessary to create a website, but they can greatly improve the chances of success and growth.

Call-to-Action

If you're ready to take the leap and start creating your own website, there's no better time to start than now! With the skills and knowledge you've gained, you can create a website that reflects your passion, your skills, or your business. So take that first step and start exploring the various platforms and tools available for website creation. With time, practice, and a little bit of patience, you can create a website that not only meets your needs, but also captivates your audience and helps you achieve your goals. So what are you waiting for? Get started today and join the millions of people around the world who are making their mark on the internet!

ϷϷϷ

NINETEEN
RENTING OUT PROPERTY OR EQUIPMENT

Generating income by renting out property or equipment can be a smart and efficient way to earn passive income. It involves putting your assets to work for you and earning money without actively participating in day-to-day operations. By identifying an asset that you own and is not being used to its full potential, preparing it for rental, and finding potential tenants, you can start earning rental income. While it may require some effort to manage the property or equipment and handle any issues that may arise, renting out assets can be a great way to generate steady passive income.

Why?

Renting out property or equipment can be a great way to earn passive income. Passive income refers to income earned without actively participating in day-to-day operations, meaning that you can generate revenue without working a traditional job. Here are some reasons why you should consider renting property or equipment as your source of income:

- **Potential for high income**: Renting out property or equipment can be an excellent source of income, particularly if you own assets in high-demand areas. Depending on the location and condition of the property or equipment, you can earn a significant amount of money that can supplement your regular income.

- **Flexibility**: Renting out property or equipment offers flexibility in terms of the amount of time and effort required. Unlike a traditional job that requires you to work a set number of hours, renting out property or equipment allows you to earn money on your own terms. This makes it an excellent option for those looking to earn extra income while also balancing other commitments.
- **Diversification of income**: Renting out property or equipment provides an excellent opportunity to diversify your sources of income. Rather than relying solely on your primary source of income, renting out property or equipment allows you to earn additional income streams that can help you achieve your financial goals and build wealth over time.
- **Use of underutilized assets:** Renting out property or equipment allows you to put underutilized assets to work, generating revenue from assets that may not be actively used. For example, if you own a second home that you only use a few weeks out of the year, renting it out can be an excellent way to earn passive income.
- **Tax benefits**: Renting out property or equipment offers numerous tax benefits, including the ability to deduct expenses related to the property or equipment from your taxes. This includes expenses related to maintenance, repairs, and upgrades, among others.

In summary, renting out property or equipment is an excellent way to earn passive income that offers a range of benefits, including flexibility, diversification of income, and tax benefits. Whether you're looking to earn extra income to supplement your regular job or build a business around renting property or equipment, this can be an excellent option to consider.

Step-by-Step Guide

Renting out property is an excellent way to earn passive income, but getting started can seem overwhelming, especially if you have limited resources. However, with some careful planning and research, anyone can successfully rent out their property and earn a steady income. Here's a step-by-step guide on how to earn money through renting property, using an example of a person with limited resources:

1. **Identify the property**: The first step is to identify the property that you want to rent out. It could be a spare room in your house, an unused garage or driveway, or a small plot of land. For this example, let's say you have a spare room in your house.

2. **Determine the rental value**: The next step is to determine the rental value of the property. You can research comparable rental prices in your area and take into account factors like location, size, and condition to determine the appropriate rental price for your property. For instance, if similar rooms in your area rent for $800 per month, you may decide to set your rental price at $750 to attract tenants.

3. **Prepare the property**: Before renting out the property, you'll need to prepare it for rental. This includes cleaning and making any necessary repairs or upgrades to the property. For our example, you may need to repaint the walls, add new curtains, and ensure that the room is clean and comfortable.

4. **Advertise the property**: Once the property is ready for rental, the next step is to advertise it. There are several online platforms such as Airbnb, VRBO, or Craigslist that can help you reach potential tenants. These platforms allow you to post details about your property and provide a secure payment gateway. In our example, the person can post the room on Craigslist or Airbnb with all the details about the rental.

5. **Set up a rental agreement**: Once you have found tenants, the next step is to set up a rental agreement. This should include details such as the rental price, security deposit, and terms of the lease. It is essential to have a well-drafted rental agreement in place to protect your interests and ensure that the tenants understand their obligations. You can create a rental agreement yourself or use a template that is available online.

6. **Collect rent and manage the property**: Once the tenants move in, you need to manage the property and collect the rent. You can either do it yourself or hire a property management company to handle these tasks for you. Property management companies take care of all the day-to-day tasks, such as collecting rent, handling maintenance and repairs, and dealing with tenant complaints and disputes. However, if you have limited resources, you may need to manage the property yourself.

7. **Be Prepared for tax obligations**: It is important to keep accurate records of all rental income and expenses, as rental income is taxable. Be sure to consult with a tax professional to understand your tax obligations and to ensure that you are in compliance with the tax laws.

In conclusion, renting out property can be an excellent way to earn some extra income, even if you have limited resources. By following the above steps, you can successfully earn money through renting out your property.

Cost and Benefit

Renting out property or equipment can be a lucrative way to earn passive income, but it also comes with its costs and benefits. On the one hand, renting out property or equipment allows you to put your assets to work for you, generating income without requiring your daily attention. This can be especially beneficial for those who have limited resources, as it allows them to earn additional income without having to make significant investments. In addition, renting out property or equipment can help offset the costs associated with owning these assets, such as maintenance and repair costs.

On the other hand, renting out property or equipment also requires some investment in terms of time and effort. Finding tenants, managing the property, and handling any issues that may arise can be a time-consuming process. Additionally, there may be legal and financial implications that need to be considered, such as taxes and insurance requirements. However, these costs can be mitigated by utilizing online rental platforms that provide assistance with legal and insurance requirements and connect landlords with potential tenants.

Overall, the cost and benefits of renting out property or equipment depend on various factors, including the type of asset being rented, the location, and the demand for that asset. With careful consideration and planning, however, renting out property or equipment can be an effective way to earn passive income and make the most of your assets.

Skills Required

Renting out property or equipment can be a profitable source of passive income, but it does require certain skills to be successful. One of the essential skills is communication. You need to be able to communicate effectively with potential renters, respond to inquiries, and negotiate rental terms. Being a good listener and understanding the needs and concerns of your tenants can help build a positive and long-term relationship.

Another important skill is organization. You need to be able to keep track of the financial aspects of your rental business, such as rental income, expenses, and taxes. You also need to be organized in terms of scheduling maintenance and repairs, managing tenant move-ins and move-outs, and keeping up with any legal or regulatory requirements.

Marketing is another key skill required to attract tenants and generate income. You need to be able to market your rental property effectively, which includes creating an appealing and accurate description, using high-quality photos, and choosing the right platforms to list your property.

Problem-solving and decision-making skills are also important when it comes to managing your rental property or equipment. You need to be able to handle unexpected issues such as maintenance or repair problems, tenant disputes, or unexpected vacancies. Being able to make quick and informed decisions can help you minimize any potential negative impact on your rental business.

Finally, being knowledgeable about real estate or the specific type of equipment you are renting is essential. This includes understanding the current market, rental trends, and legal regulations that apply to your rental business. Having a basic understanding of property maintenance, repairs, and safety issues can also be helpful in ensuring that your rental business runs smoothly and safely.

Call-to-Action

If you have property or equipment that you are not using to its full potential, consider renting it out to generate passive income. Follow the steps outlined in this guide to get started, and remember to be patient and persistent in your efforts to find tenants and manage your rentals. With the right skills and mindset, renting property or equipment can be a rewarding and profitable source of income. So why not take the first step towards financial freedom today?

ᐅᐅᐅ

TWENTY
SELLING ARTWORK

Are you an artist? Or painting is you hobby? The net revenue stream is gold for them. You can sell out your creations online.

Selling prints, photographs, and artwork refer to the commercial transaction of buying and selling reproductions of original works of art, photos, and other similar visual art pieces. These reproductions can be in the form of prints, such as giclée prints, lithographs, and screen prints. They can also be digital images, like those displayed as wall art or used for decorating purposes. The process of selling these reproductions involves a creator or artist making a copy or print of their original work and offering it for sale to the public. The buyer, in turn, purchases the reproduction for personal use, display, or as an investment. The value of these reproductions is often determined by factors such as the artist's popularity, the piece's rarity, and the print's quality.

There are several online and offline platforms in India where you can sell prints, photographs, and artwork, including:

1. **Art collectives** - Various art collectives in India bring together artists and lovers and provide a platform for selling and buying art.
2. **Online art marketplaces** - Some popular art marketplaces in India include Artisera, Artbazaar, and Indian Art Ideas.
3. **Online galleries** - Online galleries like Saatchi Art and Artsy allow you to sell your artwork globally, reaching a large audience.
4. **Gallery representation** - You can also seek representation from a local gallery in your city to sell your artwork.
5. **Art fairs and exhibitions** - Participating in art fairs and exhibitions can provide a platform to showcase and sell your artwork.

6. **Social media** - You can also use social media platforms like Instagram and Facebook to showcase and sell your artwork.
7. **Direct sales** - You can sell your prints, photographs, and artwork directly to customers through your website, email, or in-person sales.

Why?

Selling prints, photographs, and artwork in India can be a good option for several reasons:

1. **Growing art market:** The art market in India has been growing steadily in recent years and there is increasing demand for high-quality prints, photographs, and artwork from both local and international buyers.
2. **Diverse audience:** India has a rich cultural heritage and a diverse audience with a keen interest in art, making it an ideal market for selling prints, photographs, and artwork.
3. **Large talent pool:** India has a large pool of talented artists, photographers, and graphic designers, which can provide a constant source of new and innovative work for buyers to choose from.
4. **Affordable prices:** Compared to many other countries, the prices of prints, photographs, and artwork in India are relatively low, making them accessible to a wider range of buyers and providing opportunities for artists and photographers to reach a larger audience.
5. **Growing online market:** The growth of e-commerce in India has made it easier for artists and photographers to reach a wider audience by selling their work online, which has increased the demand for prints, photographs, and artwork.

These factors, along with the growing interest in art and photography in India, make it a promising market for selling prints, photographs, and artwork.

Steps to Start

Here are some steps you can follow to start selling prints, photographs, and artwork:

1. **Determine your target market:** Identify the types of prints, photographs, and artwork you want to sell and determine your target market. Research what types of art are popular with your target audience and their buying habits.
2. **Create a portfolio:** Compile a collection of your best work and create a portfolio to showcase your skills and style. You can use platforms like Behance or Flickr or create a website specifically for your art.
3. **Set prices:** Determine your prints, photographs, and artwork prices. Consider the cost of materials, printing, and shipping when setting your prices. You can also research prices of similar pieces by other artists to get a sense of the market.
4. **Choose a platform to sell your work:** There are many online platforms you can use to sell your prints, photographs, and artwork, such as Society6, Fine Art America, or Etsy. Consider each platform's fees, payment options, and shipping policies before making a decision.
5. **Market your work:** Use social media, email marketing, and other marketing techniques to promote your work to your target audience. You can also participate in local art fairs and exhibitions to get your work in front of new audiences.
6. **Follow up with customers:** After a sale, follow up with your customers to ensure they are satisfied with their purchase. This will help build a loyal customer base and encourage repeat business.
7. **Continuously improve your skills and portfolio:** Keep learning new techniques, expanding your skills, and updating your portfolio regularly to stay relevant and attract new customers.

Cost-Benefit Analysis

Following these steps, you can start selling your prints, photographs, and artwork and grow your business.

Costs

- **Production costs:** This includes the cost of materials, equipment, and labor involved in creating the prints, photographs, and artwork.
- **Marketing costs:** This includes the cost of advertising, promotions, and events to create awareness and drive sales of your products.

- **Shipping costs**: This includes the cost of packaging and shipping the prints, photographs, and artwork to customers.
- **Website/E-commerce platform costs** include setting up and maintaining an online store or website to sell your products.

Benefits

- **Revenue generation:** The primary benefit of selling prints, photographs, and artwork is generating revenue through selling your products.
- **Increased exposure:** Selling your products online or through exhibitions can increase exposure and build brand recognition.
- **Diversification of income streams:** Selling prints, photographs, and artwork can diversify your income streams and provide a source of passive income.
- **Customer feedback:** Selling your products can provide valuable customer feedback, which can inform future product development and improve the overall quality of your work.

In conclusion, the cost-benefit analysis for selling prints, photographs, and artwork will depend on various factors, such as production scale, marketing expenses, and the target market. It's essential to carefully weigh the costs and benefits before deciding to sell your products.

Skills Required

To be successful in selling prints, photographs, and artwork, several skills are essential to have:

- **Artistic vision:** Understanding what is visually appealing and having a solid sense of your style can help you produce and select pieces that will sell.
- **Marketing skills:** You must effectively market your work to potential customers and promote yourself and your brand.
- **Networking:** Building relationships with galleries, art buyers, and other industry professionals can help you get your work in front of the right people.
- **Business acumen:** Knowing how to run a business, including pricing your work, handling finances, and managing your operations, is

essential for success in this field.

- **Technological proficiency:** Familiarity with digital tools and platforms can help you display your work online and reach a wider audience.
- **Communication skills:** You need to clearly articulate your work's value to potential buyers and negotiate prices effectively.
- **Passion:** A genuine love for art and a desire to share your work with others are critical components of success in this field.

In addition to these skills, it can be helpful to have a strong understanding of the art world, including the history of photography and art movements, as well as a knowledge of the market and current trends.

"Bring Art to Life: Upgrade Your Space with Stunning Prints, Photographs, and Artworks Today!

Selling your prints, photographs, and artwork can be an incredibly rewarding experience, both financially and emotionally. Not only will you be able to monetize your creativity and hard work, but you'll also be able to share your vision and inspire others with your art. Additionally, selling your art can also give you the opportunity to connect with a wider audience, as well as establish yourself as a professional artist. Furthermore, selling your prints and artwork can help you build a name for yourself, increase your exposure, and provide you with valuable feedback from your customers. Selling your prints, photos, and artwork is a terrific way to transform your hobby into a lucrative and satisfying business, to put it briefly.

ppp

Epilogue

Congratulation on completion of this book!

In this book, we have explored a variety of ways to make money online. From starting a blog to creating an online course, there are numerous options available for people of different skill sets and interests. We have discussed the pros and cons of each method, as well as provided step-by-step guides and resources to help you get started. Whether you're looking for a side hustle or a full-time income, there is something in here for everyone.

Remember that success in any of these endeavors requires hard work, patience, and perseverance. The online world is constantly evolving, so it's important to stay up to date with the latest trends and tools. By following the tips and strategies outlined in this book, you'll be on your way to achieving your financial goals and creating a successful online business.

In this book, we have explored a variety of ways to make money online. From starting a blog to creating an online course, there are numerous options available for people of different skill sets and interests. We have discussed the pros and cons of each method, as well as provided step-by-step guides and resources to help you get started. Whether you're looking for a side hustle or a full-time income, there is something in here for everyone.

Remember that success in any of these endeavors requires hard work, patience, and perseverance. The online world is constantly evolving, so it's important to stay up to date with the latest trends and tools. By following the tips and strategies outlined in this book, you'll be on your way to achieving your financial goals and creating a successful online business.

In conclusion, the opportunities for making money online are endless, and the above list is just the tip of the iceberg. Whether you are looking to start a side hustle, make some extra cash, or turn your passion into a full-time career, there is something out there for everyone. The key is to be proactive, creative, and persistent. Don't be afraid to take risks, make mistakes, and learn from them. Remember, success is not an overnight journey, but with hard work and dedication, you can achieve anything you set your mind to. So, what are you waiting for? Go out there, explore your options, and take the first step towards your financial freedom today!In conclusion, the opportunities for making money online are endless, and the above list is just the tip of the iceberg. Whether you are looking to start a side hustle, make some extra cash, or turn your passion into a full-time career, there is something out there for everyone. The key is to be proactive, creative, and persistent. Don't be afraid to take risks, make mistakes, and learn from them. Remember, success is not an overnight journey, but with hard work and dedication, you can achieve anything you set your mind to. So, what are you waiting for? Go out there, explore your options, and take the first step towards your financial freedom today!

www.ingramcontent.com/pod-product-compliance
Lightning Source LLC
Chambersburg PA
CBHW070900160726
48004CB00003B/1183